Michael M. Dediu

World
Constitution
Implementation

Moving from violent changes, to
smooth transition to the
Constitution of the World

DERC Publishing House

Nashua, New Hampshire, U. S. A.

Published and printed in the
United States of America
On the Great Seal of the United States are included:
E Pluribus Unum (Out of many, one)
Annuit Coeptis (He has approved of the undertakings)
Novus Ordo Seclorum (New order of the ages)

Library of Congress Control Number: 2020909629

Dediu, Michael M.

World Constitution Implementation
Moving from violent changes, to smooth transition to the
Constitution of the World

ISBN-13: 978-1-950999-14-9

MSG0372548_5Oe0066V622256p32Jgi
1-8873271001
1-42QWZR8
26P1RFO5

Preface

For thousands of years, wars and violence were used to change something in the world – now, finally, all people will have a smooth, peaceful and harmonious transition to the new Constitution of the World, just published on 7 March 2020.

The big family of over 7.7 billions of people living on Earth want a good and friendly implementation of this new, sharp, clear, nonviolent and sustainable Constitution of the World, which will finally eliminate wars, nuclear arms, and many other deadly habits of the past.

Celebrating this year 250th anniversary of Ludwig van Beethoven fits perfectly with having this new lovely Constitution, which will start the next 10,000 years of harmony.

In this book we present this pleasant implementation of the new Constitution of the World, which, finally, will create the conditions for a pacific, free and prosperous new country, Peaceful Terra.

Michael M. Dediu, Ph. D.

Nashua, New Hampshire, U. S. A., 27 May 2020

USA, New York: On 7th Avenue at West 57th Street, looking southwest: right: a classical building, which is tangent to the right, on W 57th St, to the American Fine Arts Society building (1892); left down: a beautiful building, opposite Carnegie Hall (to the left, across 7th Ave, 1891, concert hall with exceptional acoustics, architecture and performance history); left up: an impressive double skyscraper, with the southwest side on W 56th St.

Table of Contents

Italy, Rome (753 BC, one of the oldest cities in Europe, called Roma Aeterna (The Eternal City) and Caput Mundi (Capital of the World)), from the Pincian Hill looking southwest: Piazza del Popolo (1822), with the Egyptian obelisk (36 m) of Sety I (1290–1279 BC) and Rameses II (1303, 1279–1213 BC) from Heliopolis, brought in 10 BC by Augustus (63 BC-14 AD) for Circus Maximus, in 1589 here. Basilica San Pietro (1506, 132 m, back).

1. Objectives

SUN: What a nice Constitution of the World you have!

EARTH: Thank you, we needed this Constitution for long….

SUN: Now comes the beautiful part – the transition from the status quo, with lots of complications, to the new Constitution.

EARTH: Which is so nice and peaceful – yes, you are right, we have to work on a smooth and friendly transition.

SUN: How do you start it?

EARTH: As you know, the first step is important and sometimes a little more difficult, but the plan is clear: we need to start with the most difficult issue, which is also the first objective of the Constitution - completely eliminate war and any type of conflicts.

SUN: Well, easy to say….

EARTH: True, but some good people in the past tried to do some reductions of armaments, and they actually had some success – we will build on this, and will do much better. We will start with small meetings between the major military powers, to immediately begin the elimination of all nuclear arms. Then, step by step, all the countries will begin to eliminate all war-related equipment.

France, Paris: Place de la Concorde: the north side of the Egyptian obelisk (circa 1250 BC), with hieroglyphics about the pharaoh Ramses the Great (1303 BC – 1213 BC (90 years), reign 1279 BC – 1213 BC (66 years)). The obelisk is from Luxor, rises 23 m, weights 250 t and it was placed here by the King Louis Philippe I (1773 – 1850, reign 1830 – 1848) in 1836, On the pedestal are drawn diagrams showing the techniques used for transportation. The original cap was stolen in Luxor around 550 BC, and the French Government added a gold-leafed pyramid cap in 1998.

SUN: Good start for a peaceful and harmonious world.

EARTH: Yes, people want peace and harmony, and they will have exactly what they want – nobody can stop this process.

SUN: That's right!

EARTH: After eliminating all arms, naturally the people will move to consolidate a peaceful and harmonious world by implementing the new Constitution.

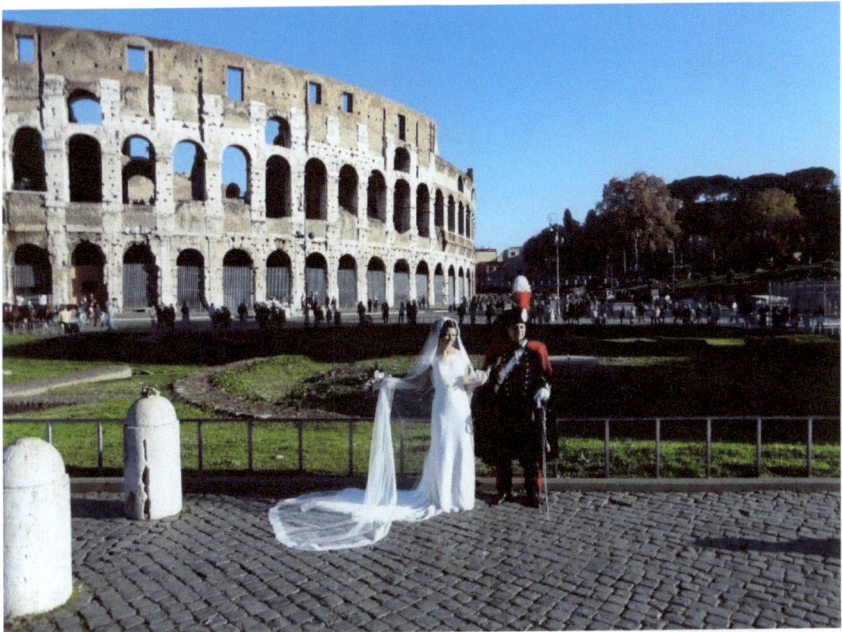

Rome: The south-west side of the Amphitheatrum Flavium (Colosseum, 80 AD) and a carabiniere wedding photo event.

2. Freedom, dignity, good families and respect

SUN: No question that all people want freedom, dignity, good families and respect.

EARTH: And this will become reality by rapidly implementing the new Constitution, which gives all the practical instruments for accomplishing these objectives.

Switzerland, Geneva (121 BC under Romans, 375 m elevation), Quai Gustave Ador at Rue du 31 Décember (right), from the road to the Jet d'Eau.

3. Good health

SUN: Having good health and good education are sine qua non requirements for all people.

EARTH: Indeed, the coronavirus pandemic is one more example why the new Constitution needs to be quickly implemented.

SUN: Yes, it has a clear description of the many medical improvements which are needed.

EARTH: In order to avoid future pandemics, the new Constitution must be firmly in place.

USA, Boston: 3 Dec 2009, Brigham and Women's Hospital (1980, three old hospitals merged) at 221 Longwood Avenue (right).

4. Friendly atmosphere and prosperity

SUN: A friendly atmosphere and prosperity is everybody's dream.

EARTH: And we will not stop until this dream becomes a reality, and the new Constitution is unquestionably the necessary tool to arrive there quickly.

The move to a much better one country on Earth is not a sprint - it is a long, steady and pleasant marathon. Burnout may come for some leaders, because isn't just about keeping a ship afloat, but it's about not always having full control. Studies have shown that the loss of control is a big stressor. To work the longest hours and to bear the greatest burden is not so effective. Having clear priorities and reserving energy are important. Delegate, walk. outside, in the Sun, for half an hour or more. Sleep at least 7 hours/night, also Meditate in a positive way, and show gratitude. Narcissistic leaders are not good, avoid logistics chaos, collaborate with NGOs and local governments in new ways, and always be a people-focused leader.

5. World Government

SUN: To me, it is obvious that the World Government must have the safety and wellbeing of all the people in the world as the highest priority.

EARTH: Yes, indeed, all people agree on this idea – there must be a constant effort to implement this idea, using the new Constitution.

Italy, Rome (753 BC), Villa Borghese (1630), Lake Garden, from Viale del Lago, Tempio di Esculapio (1786, Temple of Asclepius (god of medicine, healing, rejuvenation and physicians)) on artificial island; on front, in Greek "To Asclepius the savior".

6. Peaceful-oriented results and experience

SUN: Over the last several thousands of years, I noticed that people on Earth accumulated a good amount of peaceful-oriented results, experience and knowledge.

EARTH: Certainly, we need to use all this good amount of peaceful-oriented results, experience and knowledge, for a much better future, and the Constitution will give us all the necessary structure to achieve this objective.

Switzerland, Geneva (121 BC under Romans, 375 m elevation), Quai Gustave Ador at Rue du 31 Décembre (left), from the road to the Jet d'Eau.

7. Total area

SUN: Having a total area of over 509 M km^2, and land area over 148 M km^2 is pretty nice for a country.

EARTH: Well, you cannot ask for more – and in the future we'll expand to the Moon, asteroids, Mars, etc.

Italy, Venezia: Ponte dell'Accademia, with Accademia di Venezia (left), Palazzi Gambara and Contarini degli Scrigni (center), south bank.

8. Short common-sense rules

SUN: Not more than 2,000 rules, on maximum 1,000 pages, would be a great achievement.

EARTH: Yes, from a hyperinflation of bureaucratic rules and regulations, we'll come to several short common-sense rules, in less than 5 months.

Switzerland, Geneva, Port Miniature on Lac Léman (372 m elevation) and Jet d'Eau – a large fountain pumping water at 0.5 m^3/s to 140 m.

9. Ten simple and friendly regions

SUN: Having 10 simple and friendly regions of around 770 M people each is really good for better administration.

EARTH: Yes, this will require intense and friendly work of many people, with the help of the United Nations, and the results will be astonishing and much celebrated. Let's mention now that Earth Day is on 22 April, World Book Day is on 23 April, and that the World Ocean is very important for all the people.

Italy, Venezia: Palazzi Gritti (left) and Ferrofini (center), with Rio dell'Albero between them, across from S. Maria Della Salute.

10. Bern, Libreville (Gabon) and Oxford (UK)

SUN: Region R0 between meridians 0 and 15^0 E, with capitals in Bern (Switzerland) and Libreville (Gabon), and assistance from Oxford (UK) is a good beginning.

EARTH: Yes, it has parts of western Europe and central-western Africa.

Oxford, UK: On Oriel Street, looking to the west façade of Oriel College (1326), Merton St, Corpus Christy College (1517, right).

11. Warsaw, Pretoria (South Africa), Miami (USA)

SUN: The region R1: 15^0 E - 30^0 E, with capitals at Warsaw (Poland), and Pretoria (South Africa), and assistance from Miami (FL, USA) is attractive.

EARTH: Yes, the distance between Warsaw (Poland) and Pretoria (South Africa) is over 8,800 km, and from Pretoria to Miami is about 13,000 km – it gives a good world perspective.

Paris, France: Monument to Frédéric Chopin (1810-1849, composer) in Parc Monceau (1779, 8.2 ha), on Boulevard de Courcelles.

12. Moscow, Cairo (Egypt), Grenoble (France)

SUN: The region R2 between 30^0 E and 45^0 E has capitals in Moscow (Russia) and Cairo (Egypt), with friendly assistance from Grenoble (France) -they look to me close to an equilateral geodesic triangle.

EARTH: Yes, indeed, Moscow to Cairo is over 2,800 km, from Cairo to Grenoble over 2,700 km, and from Grenoble to Moscow over 2,500 km.

Rome: Trajan's column (113, center-left), la Chiesa Santissimo Nome di Maria al Foro Traiano. The columns were part of Basilica Ulpia.

13. Nur-Sultan (Kazakhstan), Karachi, Montpellier

SUN: This R3 region, between meridians 45^0 E and 75^0 E is also interesting, with its first capitals at Nur-Sultan (or Astana, Kazakhstan) and Karachi (Pakistan), the kind assistance coming from Montpellier (France).

EARTH: Nur-Sultan (or Astana, Kazakhstan) to Karachi (Pakistan) is about 3,000 km, and Karachi to Montpellier (France) is about 6,000 km.

Switzerland, Geneva (121 BC under Romans), Avenue de la Paix 19, International Committee of the Red Cross founded by Jean Henri Dunant (1828-1910) on Feb. 9, 1863, three Nobel Peace Prizes.

14. New Delhi, Novosibirsk, Magdeburg (Germany)

SUN: Look at this nice region R4, between 75^0 E and 85^0 E, with capitals at New Delhi (India) and Novosibirsk (Russia), collaborating with Magdeburg (Germany).

EARTH: Yes, really nice: New Delhi (India) to Novosibirsk (Russia) is about 3,000 km, and New Delhi to Magdeburg (Germany) is about 5,900 km.

Italy, Venezia: Palazzo Gritti, Canal's north bank, 550 m west from San Marco.

15. Krasnoyarsk, Űrümqi (China), Avignon

SUN: Now comes the attractive region R5: 85^0 E - 100^0 E, with its first capitals at Krasnoyarsk (Russia) and Űrümqi (China), working with Avignon (France).

EARTH: Krasnoyarsk (Russia) to Űrümqi (China) is about 1,400 km, and Űrümqi to Avignon (France) is over 6,300 km.

Cambridge, UK: From the King's Parade, looking southwest to the east façade of the entrance of King's College (1441, by King Henry VI (1421-1471)).

16. Jakarta (Indonesia), Beijing (China), Neuchâtel

SUN: The region R6: 100^0 E - 115^0 E, with capitals in Jakarta (Indonesia) and Beijing (China), and friendly assistance from Neuchâtel (Switzerland) is really inspiring.

EARTH: I agree, Jakarta (Indonesia) to Beijing (China) is over 5,200 km, and Neuchâtel (Switzerland) to Beijing is over 8,000 km.

Italy, Venezia: Palazzo Cavalli Franchetti, with Rio dell'Orso and Palazzo Barbaro (right) and Ponte dell'Accademia (left).

17. Tokyo, Sydney (Australia), Malmö (Sweden)

SUN: This nice region R7: 115^0 E - 180^0 has capitals in Tokyo (Japan) and Sydney (Australia), with kind help from Malmö (Sweden).

EARTH: Yes, Tokyo (Japan) to Sydney (Australia) is over 7,800 km, and Sydney to Malmö (Sweden) is over 16,000 km.

Switzerland, Geneva (121 BC under Romans, 375 m elevation), United Nations seen from Avenue de la Paix.

18. Washington, Mexico City, Bellinzona (Switzerl.)

SUN: This lovely region R8: 180^0 - 70^0 W has capitals in Washington (USA) and Mexico City (Mexico), with inspiring help from Bellinzona (Switzerland).

EARTH: Sure, Washington (USA) to Mexico City (Mexico) is over 3,000 km, and Mexico City to Bellinzona (Switzerland) is about 9,600 km.

Italy, Venezia: Ponte dell'Accademia. Left: Palazzi Gambara, Contarini degli Scrigni, Loredan, Moro. Right: Giustinian-Lolin, Falier.

Switzerland: Geneva (121 BC under Romans, 375 m elevation, population 200,000, area 16 km^2, 70 km northwest of Mont Blanc (4810 m)), on Rue de la Servette (to the right, Rue Jean Robert Chouet ((1642-1731, physician and politician) (the street is to the left, going northeast)), a nice building having down the restaurant Le Portail Chez Rui (yellow), 1.6 km northwest from Jet d'Eau, 1.6 km southwest from Palais des Nations (UN), 1.4 km northwest from the Université de Genève (1559, John Calvin (1509-1564)).

19. Halifax (Canada), Brasilia, Biel (Switzerland)

SUN: Finally, the fascinating 10th region R9: 70^0 W – 0 has capitals in Halifax (Canada) and Brasilia (Brazil), with friendly assistance from Biel (Switzerland).

EARTH: Yes, indeed, Halifax (Canada) to Brasilia (Brazil) is over 6,900 km, and from Brasilia to Biel (Switzerland) is over 8,800 Km.

Italy, Venezia: Palazzi Corner (Ca' Granda) (Prefettura) (left), Gritti (center-left) and Ferrofini (right), with Rio dell'Albero between them, 520 m.

20. One hundred sub-regions S00,...., S99

SUN: Then, each of the 10 regions will be divided by meridians in 10 sub-regions S00,...., S99, each with about 77 M people – this will certainly require some good work.

EARTH: No question – but local competent administrators, with some help from the capitals and others, will find good practical delimitations between very friendly sub-regions, each with about 77 M people. The delimitations will be flexible, in order to maintain a relatively constant 77 M people.

France: On the road close to Sallanches.

21. One thousand districts D000, D001,..., D999

SUN: When you go farther to each of the 100 sub-regions to be divided in 10 districts D000, D001,..., D999, each with about 7.7 M people, the local details become more important.

EARTH: Indeed, and each of the districts will have their current small and big cities. Detailed work will be necessary at local level, with help from outside, but everybody is interested in better life and harmony. Having telework, many people will have a northern residence and a southern residence, seasonally moving from one to the other, to avoid extreme cold or heat, and having the same hour.

Italy, Venezia: Palazzo Grassi, and Fermata San Samuele (right), Canal's north bank, north direction, 1.25 km west from San Marco.

22. Free navigation

SUN: The good news is that all the oceans will belong to all the regions, therefore will be managed and maintained by those regions, to be free of any piracy or other bad activity.

EARTH: Sure, and the World Police will help when necessary. Free navigation and free use of the oceans will be guaranteed for all people.

Switzerland, Geneva (121 BC under Romans, 375 m elevation), Quai du Mont Blanc going southwest, 1 km northwest of Jet d'Eau (a large fountain pumping water at 0.5 m3/s to 140 m, lit up at night), with a Franck Muller Boutique (right, watch manufacturer).

23. No borders

SUN: Finally, after waiting many thousands of years, my Peaceful Terra will have no borders.

EARTH: Yes, indeed, there will be just simple administrative delimitations, and all these delimitations between regions, as well as between sub-regions, will be flexible – they will be changed after each census (5 years), for maintaining a balanced number of people in all regions (around 770 M), and sub-regions (around 77 M).

Italy, Rome, Forum Caesaris (46 BC, by Julius Caesar (100 – 44 BC), with Temple of Venus Genetrix (center)), Via dei Fori Imperiali (left), Chiesa dei Santi Luca e Martina (right, 625, 1669).

24. First implementation

SUN: As expected, in the first implementation, as you presented above, there are many big differences between the populations of different regions, and then between the populations of different sub-regions.

EARTH: No question about it, but this is just the first implementation, which needs to be quickly put in place, and then, very easily, the administrative delimitations will be moved a few kilometers east or west, to reach a balanced population. Because all the people are in the same country, it is normal to modify a little its regions, for better administration, to make everybody happy. It is well understood that there will be some difficulties in the beginning, like in all beginnings, but with calm, patience, perseverance and hard work, the things will improve fast, and all the people will enjoy a better life.

France: Lyon (43 BC), the northwest corner of Place Louis Pradel (1906 – 1976, politician from Lyon), northwest of Opéra National de Lyon.

25. Four levels of world management

SUN: Now let's talk about the Government of my Peaceful Terra

EARTH: With great pleasure - the family of over 7. 7 B people on Peaceful Terra will have four levels of world management; however, at the local level, if needed, it could be one or two more levels of local managers (mayors, town managers, county managers – let me repeat: all levels of management must be friendly, helpful, fast, polite, modest and smart).

Switzerland, Geneva (121 BC), an elegant building on Boulevard Georges Favon

25.1. Level 1 Management

SUN: You have Level 1 Management, with 1,000 L1 friendly managers.

EARTH: Yes, I am proud of these devoted 1,000 L1 friendly managers for the 1,000 districts on Earth. They will supervise and assist the mayors and town managers from their district, for a total of about 7,700,000 people in each district. Each of the 1,000 L1 friendly managers will be located in a central city from their districts – some could be the mayors of those cities, but with new responsibilities for the whole district.

Italy, Venezia: Procuratie Vecchie (circa 1520, left), Basilica di San Marco (828 – 1071, back), Campanile (1156, restored 1514, rebuilt 1912, right).

25.2. Level 2 Management

SUN: What about the Level 2 Management, with 100 L2 friendly managers?

EARTH: All 100 L2 friendly managers for the 100 sub-regions, who will supervise and assist the 10 L1 managers of the 10 districts of each sub-region, for a total of about 77,000,000 people for each sub-region, are ready. These 100 L2 friendly managers will move each month between the two capitals of each of the 100 sub-regions.

France, Paris, the north-west part of L'Institut de France (1795, moved in 1805 by Napoléon in this baroque building from 1684) is a revered French cultural society with five académies, the most famous being Académie Français (1635) and. Académie des sciences (1666).

From Paris to Abuja

SUN: Let's see the first 5 sub-regions of R0.

EARTH: - The sub-region R00 will have the capitals Paris (France) and Niamey (Niger) – assistance from Magdeburg (Germany).
- The sub-region R01 will have the capitals Brussels (Belgium) and Porto-Novo (Benin) - assistance from Toronto (Canada).
- The sub-region R02 will have the capitals Amsterdam (Netherlands) and Algiers (Algeria) - assistance from Graz (Austria).
- The sub-region R03 will have the capitals Luxembourg (Luxembourg) and Sao Tome (Sao Tome and Principe) - assistance from Adelaide (Australia).
- The sub-region R04 will have the capitals of Abuja (Nigeria) and Bochum (Germany) - assistance from Nikko (Japan).

    The practical implementation of all these sub-regions is really easy – for example, for R00, the mayor from the assistance city Magdeburg (Germany) sends kind e-mails to the mayors of Paris and Niamery, inviting them to start the discussions, and to propose the initial delimitations of R00, within 3 days. Then friendly discussions about the details will also include the neighboring sub-regions R01 and R99, and within 3 days they will decide the delimitations of R00, which will not be perfect, but good enough to start the delightful process of building the sub-regions of a brand new and much better single country. Then they will immediately start to work to improve the living standards of all their people, by establishing a list of priorities. Weekly and monthly reviews will help to improve their initial plans, and work will continue in an atmosphere of collaboration and friendship. When difficulties appear, assistance will be requested from medical and other assistants, as well as from the upper management. No conflicts of any nature are acceptable. As in any big family, all will work in peace and harmony, for the benefit of all people.

Italy, Roma (753 BC, one of the oldest occupied cities in Europe, called Roma Aeterna (The Eternal City) and Caput Mundi (Capital of the World)), southeast of Piazza del Popolo (1822, by Giuseppe Valadier, inside the northern gate in the Aurelian Walls, the Porta Flaminia, now called the Porta del Popolo), near Via del Babuino (opened in 1525 as the Via Paolina) and the church Santa Maria in Montesanto (1679, begun by Rainaldi and completed by Bernini and Fontana), the statue of the Goddess of Abundance.

From Zürich to N'Djamena

SUN: Good and clear details. Let's see now the next 5 sub-regions.

EARTH: - The sub-region R05 will have the capitals Malabo (Equatorial Guinea), Zürich (Switzerland) - assistance from Leeds (UK).
- The sub-region R06 will have the capitals Oslo (Norway) and Tunis (Tunisia) - assistance from Sheffield (UK).
- The sub-region R07 will have the capitals Roma (Italy) and Luanda (Angola) - assistance from Yamagata (Japan).
- The sub-region R08 will have the capitals in Berlin (Germany) and Tripoli (Libya) - assistance from New York (USA).
- The sub-region R09 will have the capitals Prague (Czech Republic) and N'Djamena (Chad) - assistance from Brisbane (Australia).

Switzerland, Geneva, Broken Chair Sculpture (1997, 2007, 12 m, 5.5 tons of wood, to protest cluster bombs & land mines) in Place des Nations.

UK, London: From the Bow Street, the northeast façade of the Royal Opera House at Covent Garden (1732, 1808, 1858, 1999, capacity 2,256). In 1734, Covent Garden presented its first ballet, Pygmalion. On 14 January 1947, the Covent Garden Opera Company gave its first performance of Carmen (1875, opera in four acts, based on a novella of the same title by Prosper Mérimée (1803-1870 (aged 67))) by French composer Georges Bizet (1838-1875 (aged 36)).

From Zagreb to Kananga

SUN: Moving now to region R1 its first great 5 sub-regions.

EARTH: - The sub-region R10 will have the capitals in Zagreb (Croatia) and Brazzaville (Congo) - assistance from Nantes (France).
- The sub-region R11 will have the capitals in Vienna (Austria), Windhoek (Namibia) - assistance from Bilbao (Spain).
- The sub-region R12 will have the capitals in Stockholm (Sweden), Bangui (Central African Republic) - assistance from Florence (Italy).
- The sub-region R13 will have the capitals in Budapest (Hungary), Rundu (Namibia) - assistance from Monaco (Monaco).
- The sub-region R14 will have the capitals in Belgrade (Serbia), Kananga (Democratic Republic of Congo) - assistance from Liverpool (UK).

Italy, Venezia: Palazzi Balbi (left), Civran-Grimani (center-right), Dandolo-Paolucci, Marcello di Leoni (right), south bank, corner to east.

From Athens to Bujumbura

SUN: The next 5 sub-regions are really interesting.

EARTH: Yes, - The sub-region R15 will have the capitals in Athens (Greece), Mongu (Zambia) - assistance from Los Angeles (CA, USA).
- The sub-region R16 will have the capitals in Helsinki (Finland) and Gaborone (Botswana) - assistance from Montreal (Canada).
- The sub-region R17 will have the capitals in Bucharest (Romania) and Gaborone (Botswana) - assistance from Philadelphia (PA, USA).
- The sub-region R18 will have the capitals in Minsk (Belarus) and Maseru (Lesotho) - assistance from Orleans (France).
- The sub-region R19 will have the capitals in Chisinau (Republic of Moldova) and Bujumbura (Burundi) - assistance from Hamburg (Germany).

France, Lyon (43 BC), part of eastern façade of the Hôtel de Ville (1645 – 1651, 1674) de Lyon, in Place de la Comédie, across Opéra.

From Kiev to Nairobi

SUN: The region R2 now – first 5 subregions.

EARTH: - The sub-region R20 will have the capitals in Kiev (Ukraine) and Kigali (Rwanda) - assistance from Ottawa (Canada).
- The sub-region R21 will have the capitals in Ankara (Turkey) and Khartoum (Sudan) - assistance from Salzburg (Austria).
- The sub-region R22 will have the capitals in Lilongwe (Malawi) and Nicosia (Cyprus) - assistance from Dallas (TX, USA).
- The sub-region R23 will have the capitals in Jerusalem (Israel) and Dodoma (Tanzania) - assistance from Strasbourg (France).
- The sub-region R24 will have the capitals in Damascus (Syria) and Nairobi (Kenya) - assistance from Stuttgart (Germany).

Rome: John Cabot University (1972), American University in Rome.

From Addis Ababa to Yerevan

SUN: I cannot wait to see the next 5 regions.

EARTH: - The sub-region R25 will have the capitals in Krasnodar (Russia) and Addis Ababa (Ethiopia) - assistance from Marseille (France).
- The sub-region R26 will have the capitals in Rostov-on-Don (Russia) and Asmara (Eritrea) - assistance from Leipzig (Germany).
- The sub-region R27 will have the capitals in Stavropol (Russia) and Djibouti (Djibouti) - assistance from Zürich (Switzerland).
- The sub-region R28 will have the capitals in Mosul (Iraq) and Moroni (Comoros) - assistance from Linz (Austria).
- The sub-region R29 will have the capitals in Yerevan (Armenia) and Baghdad (Iraq) - assistance from Göttingen (Germany).

Switzerland, Bern (1911), on Laupenstrasse at Zieglerstrasse, a nice building with La Tavola Pronta ristorante.

From Riyadh to Muscat

SUN: Obviously, region R3 surprises with its first 5 sub-regions.

EARTH: - The sub-region R30 will have the capitals in Riyadh (Saudi Arabia) and Mogadishu (Somalia) - assistance from Bonn (Germany).
- The sub-region R31 will have the capitals in Baku (Azerbaijan) and Antananarivo (Madagascar) - assistance from Le Mans (France).
- The sub-region R32 will have the capitals in Oral (Kazakhstan) and Tehran (Iran) - assistance from Pisa (Italy).
- The sub-region R33 will have the capitals in Ashgabat (Turkmenistan) and Abu Dhabi (United Arab Emirates) - assistance from Wolfsburg (Germany).
- The sub-region R34 will have the capitals in Magnitogorsk (Russia) and Muscat (Oman) - assistance from Toulouse (France).

France: Lyon (43 BC), part of eastern façade of the Hôtel de Ville (1645 – 1651, 1674) de Lyon, in Place de la Comédie, across Opéra.

From Chelyabinsk to Malé

SUN: No question that the next 5 sub-regions are fascinating.

EARTH: - The sub-region R35 will have the capitals in Chelyabinsk (Russia) and Herat (Afghanistan) - assistance from Basel (Switzerland).
- The sub-region R36 will have the capitals in Tyumen (Russia) and Kandahar (Afghanistan) - assistance from Nagoya (Japan).
- The sub-region R37 will have the capitals in Dushanbe (Tajikistan) and Labytnangi (Russia) - assistance from Limoges (France).
- The sub-region R38 will have the capitals in Astana (Kazakhstan) and Kabul (Afghanistan) - assistance from Rostock (Germany).
- The sub-region R39 will have the capitals in Islamabad (Pakistan) and Malé (Maldives) - assistance from La Rochelle (France).

Italy, Venezia: Palazzi Contadini di Figure (left), a lovely pink palazzo, north bank, corner to east, 1.2 km west of San Marco.

From Bishkek to Nagpur

SUN: Now region R4 is proud of its first 5 sub-regions.

EARTH: - The sub-region R40 will have the capitals in Bishkek (Kyrgyzstan) and Jaipur (India) - assistance from Osaka (Japan).
- The sub-region R41 will have the capitals in Akola (India) and Kashgar (China) - assistance from Genoa (Italy).
- The sub-region R42 will have the capitals in Almaty (Kazakhstan) and Coimbatore (India) - assistance from Perth (Australia).
- The sub-region R43 will have the capitals in Kuybyshev (Russia) and Agra (India) - assistance from Fukuoka (Japan).
- The sub-region R44 will have the capitals in Vertikos (Russia) and Nagpur (India) - assistance from Coral Bay (Australia).

Switzerland, Bern (1191), on Murtenstrasse, Berner Fachhochschhule, Universität Bern (1834, 15,000 students).

Japan, Osaka (which means "large hill" or "large slope", in 645 capital, 400 km west of Tokyo, the second largest city after Tokyo, metropolitan area around has 19,000,000 people, along with Paris and London is one of the most productive city in the world with a GDP of $341 billion, situated at the mouth of the Yodo River on Osaka Bay of the Pacific Ocean), a small Buddhist Temple west of Shin Osaka Washington Plaza Hotel and southwest of Shin Osaka Station (1964, 2011, 3 km from the older Osaka Station).

From Chennai to Tomsk

SUN: I am eager to see next 5 sub-regions.

EARTH: Here they are: - The sub-region R45 will have the capitals in Chennai (India) and Colombo (Sri Lanka) - assistance from Sapporo (Japan).
- The sub-region R46 will have the capitals in Lucknow (India) and Fedosikha (Russia) - assistance from Niigata (Japan).
- The sub-region R47 will have the capitals in Bilaspur (India) and Kolpashevo (Russia) - assistance from Albany (Australia).
- The sub-region R48 will have the capitals in Visakhapatnam (India) and Barnaul (Russia) - assistance from Hiroshima (Japan).
- The sub-region R49 will have the capitals in Brahmapur (India) and Tomsk (Russia) - assistance from Yokohama (Japan).

Switzerland, Bern (1191, the capital city of Switzerland, on Aare River, 140,000, 52 km², 130 km northeast of Geneva), on Bühlstrasse, at Depotstrasse (left), 150 m south of the Institut fur Rechtsmedizin der Universität Bern (1834, 15,000 students).

Italy, Venezia: The south part of the Basilica di San Marco (828 – 1071) is on the left, il Campanile (1156, restored 1514, rebuilt 1912) is in the center, and to the right there are, in order, a small part of the north part of the Palazzo Ducale (circa 820 – 1420), the north end of Jacopo Sansovino's Libreria (1537 – 1591) with Biblioteca Marciana, and the east end of the Procuratie Nuove (1582-1640), on the south side of the Piazza.

From Kathmandu to Abakan

SUN: R4 is coming strong with its first 5 sub-regions.

EARTH: - The sub-region R50 will have the capitals in Kathmandu (Nepal) and Patna (India) - assistance from Kobe (Japan).
- The sub-region R51 will have the capitals in Bayingol (China) and Novokuznetsk (Russia) - assistance from Vichy (France).
- The sub-region R52 will have the capitals in Thimphu (Bhutan) and Dhaka (Bangladesh) - assistance from Jena (Germany).
- The sub-region R53 will have the capitals in Lhasa (China) and Achinsk (Russia) - assistance from Reims (France).
- The sub-region R54 will have the capitals in Abakan (Russia) and Kumul (China) - assistance from Fribourg (Switzerland).

Switzerland, Neuchâtel, on Avenue du Premier Mars at Rue Coulon (right), the northwest side of the Université de Neuchâtel (1838, 4,400 students)

Cambridge, UK: From Trinity Ln, looking west through the entrance of Trinity Hall, (1350, by William Baterman (c 1298-1355, Bishop of Norwich between 1344 and 1355), a constituent college (the 5th oldest) of the University of Cambridge), to the Front Court and the entrance to the west building of the Front Court. To the northeast of Trinity Hall there is the separate Trinity College (1546, founder Henry VIII (1491-1547, reign 1509-1547), motto: Virtus Vera Nobilitas).

From Dibrugarh to Chiang Mai

SUN: The next 5 are so lovely.

EARTH: - The sub-region R55 will have the capitals in Kyzyl (Russia) and Dibrugarh (India) - assistance from Denmark (Australia).
- The sub-region R56 will have the capitals in Bassein (Myanmar) and Tinsukia (India) - assistance from Chiba (Japan).
- The sub-region R57 will have the capitals in Yushu City (China) and Tinskoy (Russia) - assistance from Klagenfurt (Austria).
- The sub-region R58 will have the capitals in Jiuquan (China) and Medan (Indonesia) - assistance from Lucerne (Switzerland).
- The sub-region R59 will have the capitals in Chiang Mai (Thailand) and Dehong (China) - assistance from Mulhouse (France).

Italy, Venezia: Campanile and Loggetta (left), Torre dell'Orologio (1499, back), the west façade of the Basilica di San Marco (828 – 1071, right).

From Bangkok to Ulan Bator

SUN: I am ready for the first 5 of R6.

EARTH: - The sub-region R60 will have the capitals in Bangkok (Thailand) and Kuala Lumpur (Malaysia) - assistance from Besançon (France).
- The sub-region R61 will have the capitals in Vientiane (Laos) and Singapore – assistance from Freiburg im Breisgau (Germany).
- The sub-region R62 will have the capitals in Phnom Penh (Cambodia) and Irkutsk (Russia) – assistance from Baden (Switzerland).
- The sub-region R63 will have the capitals in Palembang (Indonesia), Hanoi (Vietnam) – assistance from Thun (Switzerland).
- The sub-region R64 will have the capitals in Ulan Bator (Mongolia) and Ulan-Ude (Russia) – assistance from Chaumont (France).

Switzerland Neuchâtel, on Avenue du Premier Mars, Place Numa Droz, Quai du Port (right), a classic building with La Poste and above the upper 4 windows it is written France, Russie, Allemagne, Italie.

From Cirebon to Hong Kong

SUN: The next 5 are irresistible.

EARTH: - The sub-region R65 will have the capitals in Cirebon (Indonesia) and Nanning (China) – assistance from Vaduz (Lichtenstein).
- The sub-region R66 will have the capitals in Pontianak (Indonesia) and Baotou (China) – assistance from Lugano (Switzerland).
- The sub-region R67 will have the capitals in Surakarta (Indonesia) and Yichang (China) – assistance from Thonon-les-Bain (France).
- The sub-region R68 will have the capitals in Surabaya (Indonesia) and Changsha (China) – assistance from Burgdorf (Switzerland).
- The sub-region R69 will have the capitals in Chita (Russia) and Hong Kong (China) – assistance from Colmar (France).

Italy, Roma, Theatrum Marcelli (the Theatre of Marcellus (Marcus Claudius Marcellus, 42 BC – 23 BC, nephew of the emperor Augustus, who named this theatre after him in 11 BC)), near the Tiber river.

From Nanchang to Kupang

SUN: Let's see now the marvelous first 5 of R7.

EARTH: - The sub-region R70 will have the capitals in Bandar Seri Begawan (Brunei Darussalam) and Nanchang (China) – assistance from Turku (Finland).
- The sub-region R71 will have the capitals in Krasnokamensk (Russia) and Jinan (China) – assistance from St. Gallen (Switzerland).
- The sub-region R72 will have the capitals in Baguio City (Philippines) and Hangzhou (China) – assistance from Dole (France).
- The sub-region R73 will have the capitals in Manila (Philippines) and Taipei (Taiwan, China) – assistance from Metz (France).
- The sub-region R74 will have the capitals in Kupang (Indonesia) and Shanghai (China) – assistance from Davos (Switzerland).

France: From Geneva to Mont Blanc (4810 m) on freeway A40, near Arâches la Frasse, with Mont Blanc (center back).

From Pyongyang to Melbourne

SUN: Naturally, the next 5 sub-regions are full of splendor.

EARTH: - The sub-region R75 will have the capitals in Pyongyang (North Korea) and Seoul (South Korea) – assistance from Versailles (France).
- The sub-region R76 will have the capitals in Vladivostok (Russia) and Busan (South Korea) – assistance from Innsbruck (Austria).
- The sub-region R77 will have the capitals in Kyoto (Japan) and Khabarovsk (Russia) – assistance from Germering (Germany).
- The sub-region R78 will have the capitals in Nagoya (Japan) and Komsomolsk-on-Amur (Russia) – assistance from Venice (Italy).
- The sub-region R79 will have the capitals in Sendai (Japan) and Melbourne (Australia) – assistance from St. Moritz (Switzerland).

USA, Boston: a view of the north-east part of Boston, from Cambridge, over Charles River Basin. Federal Reserve Bank Building (187 m, left), and other tall buildings in the financial district.

From Anchorage to Hermosillo

SUN: It's time to cross the Pacific – the first 5 sub-regions of R8.

EARTH: The sub-region R80 will have the capitals in Uelen (Russia) and Anchorage (Alaska, USA), – assistance from Zug (Switzerland).
- The sub-region R81 will have the capitals in Vancouver (Canada) and San Jose (CA, USA) – assistance from Odense (Denmark).
- The sub-region R82 will have the capitals in Vernon (Canada) and Los Angeles (CA, USA) – assistance from Amstetten (Austria).
- The sub-region R83 will have the capitals in Calgary (Canada) and Tijuana (Mexico) – assistance from Chur (Switzerland).
- The sub-region R84 will have the capitals in Hermosillo (Mexico) and Tucson (AR, USA) – assistance from Bergen (Norway).

Switzerland, Neuchâtel, on Rue de la Place d'Armes, Lycee Jean Piaget (1896-1980, psychologist), Ecole Superieure Numa Droz (1844-1899, politician) & Bibliothèque publique et universitaire de Neuchâtel.

From Regina to Lima

SUN: The next 5 sub-regions will bring us to the Atlantic.

EARTH: The sub-region R85 will have the capitals in Chihuahua (Mexico) and Regina (Canada) – assistance from Gothenburg (Sweden).
- The sub-region R86 will have the capitals in San Luis Potosi City (Mexico) and Winnipeg (Canada) – assistance from Yverdon-les-Bains (Switzerland).
- The sub-region R87 will have the capitals in Tulsa (OK, USA) and Veracruz (Mexico) – assistance from Bregenz (Austria).
- The sub-region R88 will have the capitals in Memphis (TN, USA) and San José (Costa Rica) – assistance from Uppsala (Sweden).
- The sub-region R89 will have the capitals in Lima (Peru) and Boston (MA, USA) – assistance from Tampere (Finland).

Boston: 3 Dec 2009, from Harvard Medical School looking northeast to the Avenue Louis Pasteur (1822-1895, French microbiologist),

From Bangor to Cayenne

SUN: Let's see the very interesting first 5 sub-regions of R9.

EARTH: - The sub-region R90 will have the capitals in La Paz (Bolivia) and Bangor (Maine, USA) – assistance from Aosta (Italy).
- The sub-region R91 will have the capitals in Caracas (Venezuela) and Road Town (British Virgin Islands) – assistance from Obergoms (Switzerland).
- The sub-region R92 will have the capitals in Buenos Aires (Argentina) and Fort-de-France (Martinique) – assistance from Freudenstadt (Germany).
- The sub-region R93 will have the capitals in Asuncion (Paraguay) and Montevideo (Uruguay) – assistance from Winterthur (Switzerland).
- The sub-region R94 will have the capitals in Cayenne (French Guiana), St. John's (Canada) – assistance from Novara (Italy).

Switzerland, Lausanne (Roman 150, 147,000, 41 km^2, 500 m elevation), marina on Lac Léman, southwest of Place de la Navigation (right).

USA, the University of California, Berkeley (1868, named after the philosopher and mathematician Bishop George Berkeley (1685-1753), motto Fiat lux (Let there be light), 36,200 students, major public research university, 72 Nobel laureates, between the top six universities in the world, 500 ha campus), il Campanile (Sather Tower (61 bells (full concert carillon) and clock tower). 1914, 94 m, 7 floors, observation deck on the 8th floor, inspired by il Campanile (850, 1514, 1912, 99 m) di San Marco (1084), Venezia (421, Venice), Italy (900 BC)).

From Rio de Janeiro to London

SUN: Finally, pour la bonne bouche, the inviting last 5 sub-regions.

EARTH: - The sub-region R95 will have the capitals in Rio de Janeiro (Brazil) and Dakar (Senegal) – assistance from Toyama (Japan).
- The sub-region R96 will have the capitals in Freetown (Sierra Leone) and Lisbon (Portugal) – assistance from Kawasaki (Japan).
- The sub-region R97 will have the capitals in Bamako (Mali) and Athlone (Ireland) – assistance from Ulm (Germany).
- The sub-region R98 will have the capitals in Yamoussoukro (Cote d'Ivoire) and Madrid (Spain) – assistance from Okayama (Japan).
- The sub-region R99 will have the capitals in Ouagadougou (Burkina Faso) and London (United Kingdom) - assistance from Vaasa (Finland).

UK, London: From the Westminster Bridge (1862, 250 m) over Thames (flowing left to right), looking west to the Palace of Westminster (1016, 1870, left), Big Ben (Elizabeth Tower, 1855, 96 m, center right), and to Portcullis House (2001, right).

25.3. Level 3 Management

SUN: What about the management of the ten regions?

EARTH: Ten L3 friendly managers for the 10 regions will supervise and assist the 10 L2 managers of the 10 sub-regions of each region, for a total of about 770,000,000 people for each region.

Italy, Venezia, Murano: On a bridge in the south of Murano, Fondamenta Daniele Manin (right), Fondamenta dei Vetrai (left), looking north-east, towards the center of Murano.

25.4. Level 4 Management

SUN: Now let's see the top management of the world.

EARTH: Yes, the L4 level very friendly 10 Advisers of the world will supervise and assist the 10 L3 managers of the 10 regions of the Earth, for a total of over 7,700,000,000 people – all the people on Earth, citizens of Peaceful Terra.

Switzerland, Lausanne-Ouchy Ferry Terminal on Lac Léman, south of Le Château d'Ouchy (left, 1170, 1464, rebuilt 1889-1893).

Locations

SUN: And where will they be located?

EARTH: The L4 very friendly 10 Advisers of the world will be located each in one the ten Regions R0, R1,…, R9. For example, in the beginning, for the first month (then changing every month), the ten Advisers of the world will be located:

- in R0: Barcelona (Spain)
- in R1: Benghazi (Libya)
- in R2: Addis Ababa (Ethiopia)
- in R3: Hyderabad (Pakistan)
- in R4: Bhopal (India)
- in R5: Mandalay (Myanmar)
- in R6: Nanchong (China)
- in R7: Khabarovsk (Russia)
- in R8: Houston (USA)
- in R9: Recife (Brazil)

Italy, Gate 2 to the ruins of Pompeii (650 BC, in 79 covered by ash), with a panel entitled CARPE DIEM (enjoy the day), a Latin aphorism from a poem in the Odes (book 1, number 11) in 23 BC by the Roman poet Horace (Quintus Horatius Flaccus, born December 8, 65 BC in Venusia, Roman Republic, died November 27, 8 BC, in Rome, the capital of the Roman Empire). Important lyric poetry volumes are Odes, Satires and Ars Poetica.

The best management of the world

SUN: And how will they work for the benefit of all people?

EARTH: Very important indeed: these ten L4 Advisers will be in permanent contact with each other, and with the L3 Advisers, for the best management of the world.

The ten L4 Advisers will work by consensus only.

The ten L4 Advisers will be elected from the 10 regions, and each of them will be the First Adviser (*First among equals* – from Latin: Primus inter pares) for one month, by rotation.

The First Adviser only coordinates the work of the other 9 Advisors for one month.

Italy, Venezia: Libreria (left), Campanile (back), Torre dell'Orologio (back), San Theodore Column (1268), Basilica and Palazzo Ducale (right).

Mobility

SUN: Are these 10 Advisers fixed in some places?

EARTH: No, the ten L4 Advisers will move each month from a first capital of a region to the second capital of another region, at random (or based on urgency, if an emergency occurred). This mobility is essential for having a long period of tranquility and harmony.

For example, in this COVID-19 case, they all would have focused on the initial cases, help the local management to isolate the people affected, give them proper medical assistance, and stop the local travel. All the medical institutions in the world would work together to find a quick solution to this new medical problem, and, obviously, all the people would get the best protection and assistance.

3 Dec 2009, the northeast façade of the Harvard Medical School, Anno Domini 1904, founded in 1782, the graduate medical school of Harvard University (7,200 undergraduates; 14,000 Graduates, 4,671 Faculty members; 152 Nobel laureates are members of Harvard University, 12 Schools and 2 Institutes for Advanced Studies, including Harvard School of Engineering and Applied Sciences, $32.3 billion endowment. $4.2 billion budget).

26. Monthly World Report

SUN: Will these Advisors present regular short reports to the people?

EARTH: Yes, the First Adviser, on the last day of each month, will present in writing for the world (no more than 5 standard pages) a clear and precise Monthly World Report, with a list of finished and unfinished tasks. The other 9 Advisers will add their comments to the Monthly World Report (no more than half a page each - total report less than 9.5 pages).

Italy, Venezia: Monumento a Vittorio Emanuele II, with Londra Palace (back), on Riva degli Schiavoni.

26.1. Replacements

SUN: What about management and replacements?

EARTH: The top 10 Advisers will manage Police and all other Departments. For obvious uncooperative or improper attitude of one top Advisor X, the other 9 can replace X with X's number 2, and X will receive appropriate medical treatment. When vacancies happen for Advisors, the number 2 for those Advisors will fill the vacancies. All the activities of all Advisors will be recorded in computers and videos, and on paper, for people to be able to see what they are doing. Advisors at all levels should work 40 hours/week, with 4 weeks vacation, but many services (medical, police (firemen should be part of the police), emergency, volunteers) should be non-stop.

Beautiful houses in Murano, Venezia, Italy.

26.2. Spending proposals

SUN: Compensation of the world government employees is relevant.

EARTH: Yes, the world government employees will have a compensation close to the average compensation of the people in the area where they are located, but the top management will a compensation close to the world average. All Advisors are free to speak about their administrative work, but only with modesty – people will evaluate their work. All spending proposals from Advisers must be approved by their 5 assistants (doctors, mathematicians, CEOs, engineers and teachers), and must have an already existing funding in the budget.

Switzerland, Lausanne (150), Le Château d'Ouchy (tower left, 1170 by the Bishop of Lausanne, 1464, 1889-1893), hotel (center).

27. No war

SUN: Who can declare war?

EARTH: Nobody! Advisors (and all the others) cannot declare war, reprisals or capture land or water. Advisors (and all the others) cannot raise and support armies, navy, or any military forces.

Italy, Venezia: Gondole and water taxi with Danieli Excelsior (back), the second building after Palazzo Ducale on Riva degli Schiavoni.

28. Public opinion survey

SUN: Will the people be involved in the world government?

EARTH: Certainly - in order to better know the world government, to help it, and, especially, to improve it, all able people of the world will work as volunteers at least one day per year in each of the seven departments.

Also, after each Monthly World Report, a public opinion survey about the report should be taken, and presented to all Advisors. All activities of the Advisors, and others from the small World Government, will be available to the people on a website.

The top 10 Advisers (and all the others) will collaborate via e-mail, telephone, videoconferences, mail, or face to face, when needed, to produce practical results for all people, very fast.

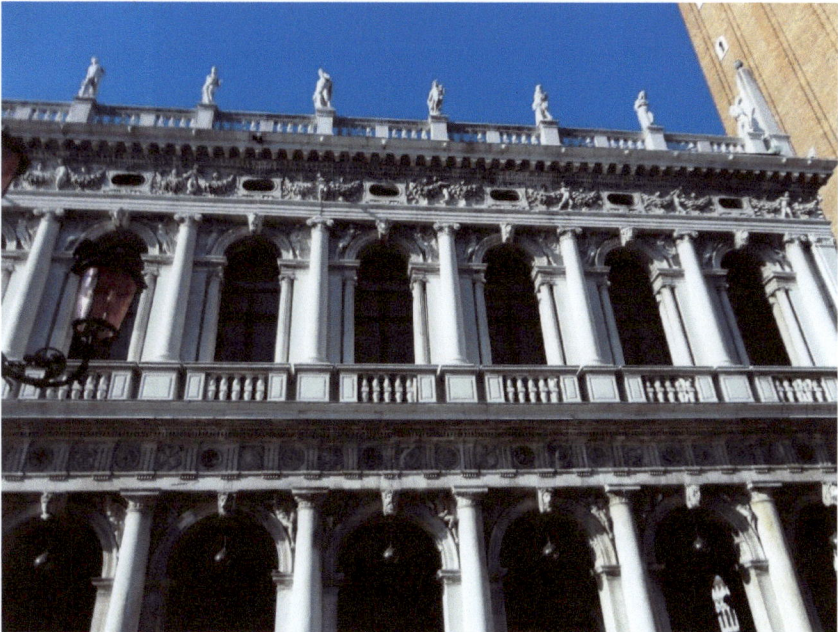

Italy, Venezia: The north part of the east façade of Sansovino's Libreria (1537 – 1591) with Biblioteca Marciana, with a part of Campanile (right).

29. Five assistants

SUN: Now, who will help the Advisors to manage the world?

EARTH: Very important indeed - each Advisor, and each manager at all levels, will have 5 immediate assistants:
1) a mathematician for finance and all other calculations,
2) a medical doctor for keeping everybody healthy, calm, polite, friendly and optimist,
3) a CEO for good management,
4) an engineer for all practical projects, and
5) a teacher for education, training and related areas.

The five assistants play a key role, because they are highly qualified professionals, who actually will carry on the practical management of the world. Their integrity, professionalism and friendliness will significantly improve the quality of the world and local governments.

The five assistants are really the experts. They will assist the Advisors and all levels of management, in order to have an efficient, correct and professional working of the world government at all levels.

Constanta, Romania, Piazza Ovidiu: Statue of Publius Ovidius Naso (20 March 43 BC, in Sulmona – 17, in Tomis, Moesia (now Constanta, Romania), aged 60.

30. Honorific World Observer

SUN: Who oversees the Advisers?

EARTH: An Honorific World Observer will be quietly elected by direct vote – starting, for example, 1st September 2022 - for only one 3 years term, with the main duty to observe that the top 10 Advisers efficiently perform their duties, and keep their words – if they don't, they will be changed.

For managers and for everybody else, keeping their word is a serious and strict requirement.

The Honorific World Observer has this responsibility for the top 10 Advisors, but all people will pay attention to this. Words must become again important and respected.

Italy, Roma: Trinità dei Monti church, 1585, with Obelisco Sallustiano (20 BC), and Scalinata della Trinità dei Monti (the Spanish Steps, 1725).

31. World Government

SUN: Let's discuss about the World Government.

EARTH: - With great pleasure - all the employees of the World Government are temporary, and must reapply for their positions every year. There is no need for unions.

The World Government will be limited to:
1) the Office of the Honorific Observer (less than 10 employees),
2) the Office of the top ten Advisors (less than 100 employees), and
3) 7 small departments, with less than 3,000,000 employees.

The number of all government employees, at all levels, will be less than 350,000,000, and at the top level less than 3,000,000.

Switzerland, Lausanne (Roman 150, 147,000, 41 km^2, 500 m elevation), marina on Lac Léman, southwest of Place de la Navigation (right).

SUN: Good numbers – let's see now the 7 departments.

EARTH: Yes, the World Government will have these 7 small departments:

31.1. Tax Department

- Collects taxes of 15% of the income of people and revenue of companies.

- The Manager of the Tax Department is appointed for a three-year term by the World 10 Advisers.

- The number of employees must be under 50,000, with excellent computers, and advanced software.

Italy, Venezia: Procuratie Vecchie (circa 1520, left), Basilica di San Marco (828 – 1071, back), Campanile (1156, restored 1514, rebuilt 1912, right).

SUN: Yes, Tax it is clear, let's see the next.

EARTH: The next is

31.2. Treasury

Treasury will control all the financial issues, including:
- antitrust
- fiscal service
- financial cooperation
- financing bank
- world reserve system
- world budget using only revenue, no borrowing, and spending only on strict necessary needs
– all the budgets, at all levels, will have a 2% surplus, which will be returned to the taxpayers
- register of all government papers and activities
- archives and records
- assist all people to have savings accounts for old age (the old age will be starting around 70), and 10% of their income should automatically go to their savings accounts. For those unable to work, their doctors and mathematicians will decide case by case.
- bankruptcies, in general, will be discouraged, and when strict necessary, will be analyzed and solved, case by case, by the doctors, mathematicians and CEOs who worked with the people who asked the bankruptcy.
- encourage all families to assist their parents, grandparents, and great-grandparents.
- housing finance
- housing for all people
- no homelessness
- consumer financial protection
- pensions
- privacy
- current social security until replaced by personal savings
- personnel management
- general services for the world government

- each the 10 regions will receive 2.5% of the world taxes - at least 30% of the money will be sent to villages and cities.

- each of the 100 sub-regions will receive 0.25% of the world taxes. At least 40% of the money will be sent to villages and cities.

- The World Central Bank will include all current central banks – starting, for example, on May 1st, 2023.

- The Special Credit Card (SCC) will be issued by the World Central Bank.

- Advisors will create a new world currency, named, for example, "coin", and all the other currencies will be exchanged for coins. The World Central Bank will implement the details.

- The counterfeiting and all other bad things, which some sick people do, will be medically treated (in specialized medical institutions when necessary), and those who did bad things will pay all the expenses, and will reimburse the victims. Victims will always be very protected, and helped to recover the losses from the attackers.

Italy, the entrance to the modern city of Pompei, located southeast of the ruins of the ancient Pompeii (650 BC, in 79 covered by ash).

SUN: Treasury has plenty of important tasks – let's see the next.

EARTH: Yes, the next Department is

31.3. People Assistance Department

It will assist people in general, including:
- parent assistance
- dispute resolution
- in very simple disputes or culpa levis (ordinary negligence, like late payments, etc.), one single assistant will decide within minutes, and all people will go back to work
- census very 5 years
- election assistance every 20 months
 - special credit cards
- people protection against abuses from anybody
- completely eliminate corruption, organized crime and drug trafficking
- all people in the world will remain in their places, and the improvements will come to them. Those who want to move to other places, will need first a special invitation from at least 10 people (not family related) where they want to move.
- all the Tribunals and related areas will be transformed in people assistance services, based on friendliness, collaboration and goodwill.
- It is well understood that no excessive bail will be required, no excessive fines imposed, no cruel and unusual punishments applied, but, at the same time, it is well understood that a person who did a bad thing will receive the necessary corrective medical treatment, and will reimburse all people who suffered damages, and the medical treatment. The victims will always receive special attention.
- Nobility (King, Prince, etc.) could continue to exist in some places, but they should not interfere with activities of the Advisors, and actually should help them.
- food safety
- trash & recycling
- free commerce
- jobs assistance

- postal service
- labor safety and harmonious relations
- land, water
- volunteers
- fitness, sport, tourism
- 10 world holidays: the normal 4 Earth events (2 solstices (around 21 June, around 21 December), and 2 equinoxes (around 21 March, around 21 September), Mother's Day on 1st May, Father's Day on 6 August, Children's Day on 6 November, Grandparents' Day on 6 February, and 2 optional days (like Thanksgiving or a Religious Day (Christmas), and New Year).

Italy, view of south of Venice, on Riva degli Schiavoni, near San Marco

SUN: Very good people assistance – let's see the next.

EARTH: Yes – the next Department is

31.4. Medical Department

It will manage all medical and healthcare related areas, including:
- human services
- conflict resolution
- families, children, elderly
- medicine approval
- disease control and prevention
- medical doctors and assistants will make regular home visits, at least once a year, to all people, to keep them healthy, and to prevent illnesses.
- medical research: cancer, heart, lung, blood, arthritis, surgical robotics, connected computers for healthcare, etc.
- healthy homes, streets, stores, working places, etc.
- healthy aging
- all misunderstandings, disagreements or conflicts of any nature will be treated by medical personnel (with police help when strict necessary), until all is back to normal.
- no prisons are necessary, only specialized medical institutions (in simple cases, the places where the treated people live can be used, with the necessary limitations and surveillance)
- If a person X is considered that did a bad thing, X will have, within 3 days, a discussion with one or more doctors and other assistants, and will be informed of the nature and cause of the bad thing; including witnesses against and for him. Then a decision will be taken within other 3 days, by a group of doctors and other assistants. Victims of bad people will always have priority to discuss their problems with one or more doctors and other assistants, and quick decisions will be taken within 3 days, by a group of doctors and other assistants. Protection of victims has always priority.
- in order to better know the world government, to help it, and, especially, to improve it, all able people of the world will work as

volunteers at least one day per year in the local facility of this department, which will have a special office for managing this volunteer work.

– all people will have government medical insurance, and they can also have private medical insurance

– there will be doctors working for the government 100%, or only part-time, or having only private practice, all with reasonable salaries and fees.

– there will be government pharmaceutical institutions and private pharmaceutical companies, offering reasonable priced medicines, without advertising to the general public.

3 Dec 2009, the northeast façade of the Harvard Medical School Anno Domini 1904, founded in 1782, the graduate medical school of Harvard University, 1660 students, acceptance rate 3.7%.

SUN: As we can see from the COVID-19 pandemic, this World Medical Department is a high priority – the sooner you have it, the better.

EARTH: Indeed, we need to work very hard for this. The next Department is

31.5. Police

Police will provide assistance for:
- accidents
- disasters
- complete elimination of nuclear, chemical and biological arms, firearms and explosives
- world complete security
- world cooperation
- conflict reduction and resolution
- investigations
- emergency assistance
- training
- delinquency prevention in general, and especially juvenile
- protection of Advisors, important government buildings, etc.
- extended surveillance and reconnaissance to prevent bad events
- fire protection
- volunteers to help police
- police will be present at public meetings, services, shows, etc., in order to protect the public
- public order
- ensuring traffic safety
- completely eliminate corruption, organized crime and drug trafficking
- movement of people based on civilized rules
- assist and protect those who have encountered violence
- World Police and specialists from the former United Nations and Interpol will be ready and very mobile for urgent and special operations, when they are needed.

- Police will be the only department which will have some small arms, in order to stop some very bad people (who are very sick).
- a small manufacturing and maintenance of arms unit will be part of the Police Department, under strict control.
- Police will work with medical personnel, mathematicians, CEOs, engineers, teachers and others, to make sure that all the people on the Planet are in good mental health, in order to prevent bad situations. This is also a major responsibility of all Advisors.
- prevention of bad events
- The Advisors will allocate the necessary budget for Police, and Police will assist people in need.

Italy, Rome (753 BC), Piazza del Campidoglio (1546 by Michelangelo, paving completed in 1940, on Collis Capitolinus, the oldest part of Rome, with Temple of Jupiter (509 BC)), a replica of the equestrian bronze statue (175, the oldest, moved here in 1538) of Marcus Aurelius (born 121, Emperor 161-180), Palazzo Senatorio (right, 1350, bell-tower 1582, atop Tabularium, now the city hall), Palazzo Nuovo (left, 1603-1654, opened 1734).

SUN: it is well-known that always there is need for Police, because of accidents, etc. And the 6th Department?

EARTH: Yes, we have the

31.6 Education Department

- Over 2 billions of children in the world will get a solid peace-oriented education, to give a solid peace-oriented foundation for a good, free, peaceful and prosperous life.
- Education is very important – teachers will work with parents and grandparents, to educate the children to leave healthy in a sustainable peace, liberty and prosperity.
- Discipline must be strict, and those who do not behave properly, will get medical assistance.
- The world will have 4 school levels (SLs) of education:
SL1 – Kindergarten – 2 years: age 5 and 6
SL2 – Primary School – 4 years: age 7, 8, 9 and 10
SL3 – Secondary School – 3 years: age 11, 12 and 13
SL4 – High School or Vocational School – 4 years: age 14, 15, 16 and 17
- A World Library will include the Library of Congress and all the other great libraries – they will remain where they are now, but will be digitally interconnected, and accessible from any place in the world.
- adult education: technical, career
- training for employment
- management training
- post high school education
- peace education
- world constitution education

Paris: view (looking south-west) of nymph statues on an Art Nouveau lamp, on the west side of Pont Alexandre III (1896-1900, for Alexander III (1845-1894), Tsar of Russia, King of Poland and Grand Prince of Finland (1881-1894)), Pont des Invalides (center – right), and the north-east side of Tour Eiffel (1889, 324 m, 279 m at the 3rd level).

SUN: No need to repeat how important the education of children is for the future of the world. And the 7th Department?

EARTH: Yes, this is relatively new:

31.7. Science & Technology Department.

It will help in the areas of:
- mathematics
- statistics
- science
- technology
- Algorithmic Governance will be an essential tool for a better and impartial governing of the world, used by the Advisers elected by people. Mathematicians from all countries will work to improve the Algorithmic Governance, to better serve the people.
- cyberspace complete security will be achieved and strictly maintained
- information systems
- computer services
- Internet
- scientific cooperation
- economic development at the world level
- infrastructure improvement and maintenance at the world level
- innovation and improvements in all areas, at the world level
- transportation at the world level
- safety
- security
- aviation
- highway
- cars
- railroads without noise
- maritime administration
- logistics
- strategic planning at the world level
- public works

- fleet maintenance
- standards: weights, measures, etc.
- research at the world level
- risk analysis
- laboratories
- engineering
communications at the world level
- telecommunications
- networks
- peaceful nuclear energy use at the world level
- safety
- waste
- electrical power
- oceanic analysis at the world level
- atmospheric analysis at the global level
- meteorological service and prognosis at the global level
- world resources analysis
- sustainable use of world resources
- geographical and geological activity
- product safety at the global level
- hazardous material and chemical safety
- government broadcasting (radio, tv, Internet, newspaper, etc.) including news, scientific and technical information
- private broadcasting will continue, but the world government must be able to directly inform the people, without intermediaries
- space exploration and expansion at the world level – very important for the future
- patent and trademark
- intellectual rights
- all government work, which can be done by private companies, will be contracted with the best and reasonably priced private companies. At the same time, the government should always have competitive services for people – from plumbing and electrical help, to mortgage and buying or selling a house.

France, Paris: La Monnaie de Paris (the Direction of Coins and Medals) created in 864 by Charles II (823-877, king 843-877), is the oldest French institution, which is still active. It also has a Musée de la Monnaie (1833), at 11 Quai de Conti, in the 6th arrondissement.

32. Elections

SUN: Well, this World Science & Technology Department is a sine qua non requirement for a modern Earth. Now some more information on elections.

EARTH: Sure. The Advisers should be elected every 20 months for one term only. If an Adviser X was elected for a term T1, then the next term T2 will have another Advisor Y. For the next term T3, X can be elected again, but the next term T4 will have a new Adviser, and so on. All levels of Advisers (minimum age 25 years) can be elected, not consecutively, at most 4 times (maximum 80 months = 6 years and 8 months).

SUN: Will the Government employees follow some well-established advice?

EARTH: Certainly - all the employees in Government will respect Seneca's (circa 1,960 years ago) aphorism "To govern is to serve, not to rule", and Hippocrates' (over 2,400 years ago) aphorism "Make a habit of two things: to help; or at least to do no harm."

SUN: Will the elections be similar to what they are now?

EARTH: Not at all - Advisers should have exceptional results obtained from their work, and based on these results, plus modesty, moderation, good character, friendliness, sharp mind, wisdom, good morals, and intense desire to help people, they will be elected, without any campaigning, publicity, fundraising, donations, debates, propaganda, political parties, advertising, or similar activities.

London, from the Shard (2012, 309 m, observatory at 244 m), looking east to the Tower Bridge (1886-1894, combined bascule and suspension turreted bridge over River Thames (flowing from west (left) to east (right)), between London boroughs Tower Hamlets (north – left up) and Southwark (south – right), length 244 m, height 65 m, longest span 82 m, clearance 8 m (closed), 42 m (open)), City Hall (2002, height 45 m, center right round, for the Greater London Authority: Mayor of London and the London Assembly)

33. Digital technology

SUN: Other details, for a smooth transition?

EARTH: Yes - there will be use of advanced digital technology, which opens up entirely new opportunities for developing direct elections, and public control of the institutions, improving the transparency of the election procedure, and taking into account the interests and opinions of each voter (over the age of 21, who are not in a special medical institution for bad behavior or for mental health).

An Election Commission of 110 representatives from the 10 regions and from the 100 sub-regions, elected separately for 5 years, will have to examine the qualifications of all the candidates for Advisers, and for other senior management positions. Unqualified candidates will be asked to improve their qualifications, and then to try again later.

It is important to refresh the management, and to bring new people to help the big family of 7.7 B people. The older generations, who performed well, will be retained in important roles, because experience and maturity count very much. At least two months before the retirement, they will kindly be asked to transfer their expertise to the younger generation. Even after retirement, they will occasionally be invited to share their expertise.

In every election, with every winner, will be other two for number 2 and number 3. The number 2 and number 3 for each management position will be used when number 1 is not available (vacation, sick, etc.). They will constantly work for number 1, helping to solve urgent problems for the people.

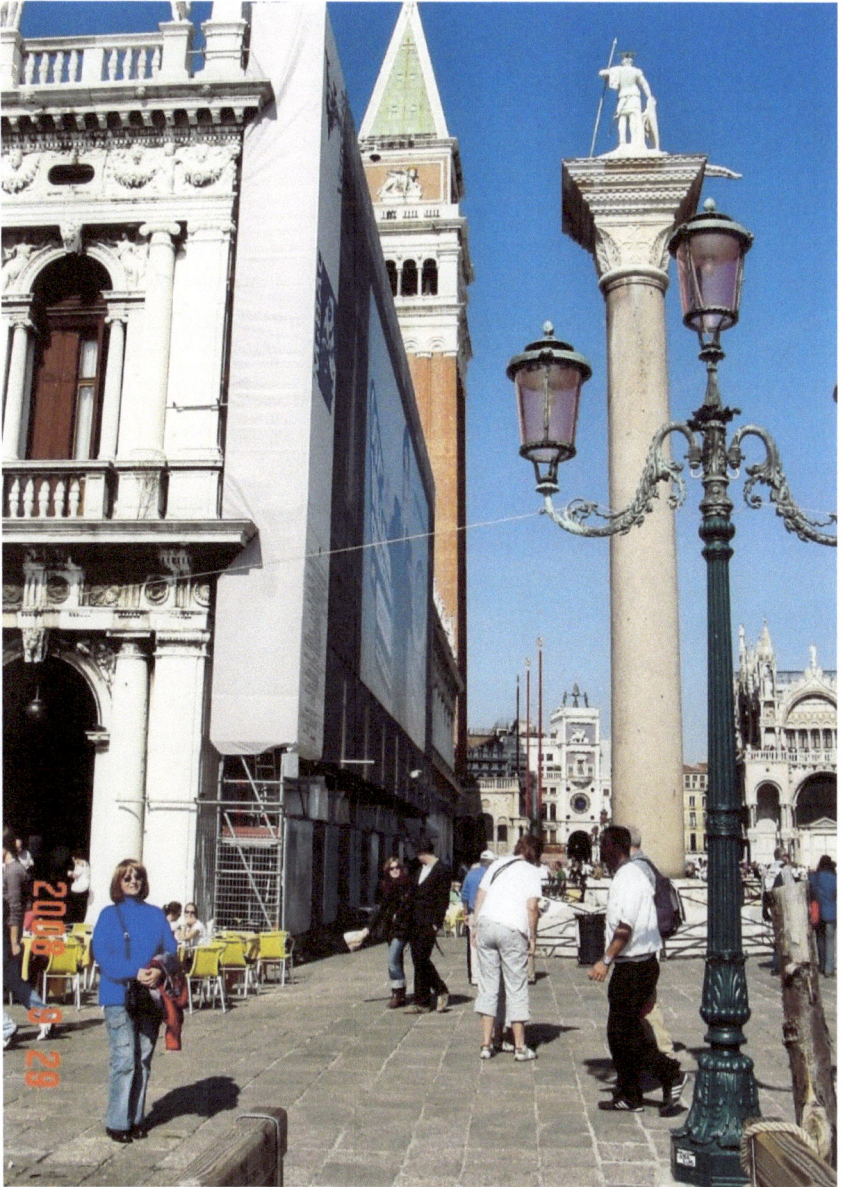

29 September 2008, Venezia (421), Piazza San Marco (1084) Libreria Sansoviniana. (1468-1560, left), Campanile (850, 1514, 1912, 99 m, back), Torre dell'Orologio (1499, back), San Theodore Column (1268), Basilica di San Marco (1156-1173, right).

34. Dediu Method

SUN: Good elections are essential for the future, and Dediu Method (as explained in this book and the previous books) is really useful.

EARTH: Indeed - there has been a tendency to make elections conflict generating events, with lots of propaganda, false information, heavy donations, unpolite confrontations, bully fundraising, hostile political parties and organizations, unlimited power ambitions, etc.

Using Dediu Method this will be completely changed into clean, friendly elections, in which people choose between leaders with outstanding results, plus talent to lead people to peace and freedom, modesty, moderation, good character, friendliness, sharp mind, wisdom, good morals, and intense desire to help people – no campaigning, no publicity, no fundraising, no donations, no debates, no propaganda, no political parties, no advertising, or similar activities.   All Advisors should also be local Administrators – they must show that they are good managers, and produce practical results for all people.

Cambridge, UK: From Trinity Lane looking to the west part of the northern façade and entrance of King's College Chapel (1446).

35. World referendum

SUN: Electronic world referendum is another essential element of Dediu Method.

EARTH: Yes, an electronic world referendum will be organized every three months. The main questions will be:

1. Are you satisfied with the Government?
2. What Government work is good?
3. What Government work is not good?
4: Suggestions for improvement:

Within two months after each referendum, the Government will respond to the people. Based on the suggestions received, new pro-people rules will be replacing some old rules.

Italy, Rome (753 BC), Forum Romanum, the northwest side of Arcus Septimii Severi (left, 203, Septimius Severus (145 – 211)), the northeast side of Templum Saturni (center, 497 BC, 42 BC, 380), Tabularium (right up, 78 BC by Lucius Cornelius Sulla).

36. Complete disarmament

SUN: Total and complete disarmament is a fundamental element of Dediu Method.

EARTH: Yes, arms will not exist anymore, and only the police will have some small arms. Those who want arms for hunting or sport, will borrow them from police stations, with proper documents, rules and payments.

All military units will become strong civilian organizations, working to improve the quality of life for everybody.

For practical reasons, the transition from the current imperfect situation to the much better Sustainable Peace and Prosperity Structure (SPPS) will be very smooth: first - all the countries remain as they are, and they will begin – for example on January 1st, 2021 - to negotiate total and complete disarmament, with the help of the United Nations, for 3 months. Then for 5 months will intensely work to eliminate all the arms – either transform them in peaceful tools, or destroy them. Then a continuous verification and monitoring will be implemented, to make sure that the world finally achieved complete disarmament forever!

37. Census

SUN: What about census?

EARTH: A census will take place every 5 years – starting, for example, on October 1st, 2023 - and now we apply Dediu Method: all people will receive a special credit card (SCC), with their photo and other personal data. The delimitations between regions, and between sub-regions, will be adjusted by the census.

London: The northwest façade of the Old Vic Theatre (1818, 1871, 1902, 1927, 1938, 1950, 1960, 1963, 1985, 2003, 1067 capacity), on the corner of The Cut and Waterloo Rd., a traditional playhouse with big name actors (Laurence Olivier (1907-1989)) and top directors.

38. Special credit card

SUN: The special credit card (SCC) is another important element of Dediu Method.

EARTH: Yes, the special credit card (SCC) will be used to buy everything, to identify for voting, for census, for travel, for medical assistance, etc. The current private credit cards will continue to work as usual. The changes of the delimitations between regions, and also sub-regions, will be inputted on these cards, and no other work is needed.

Switzerland, Lausanne (150), Place de la Navigation, the south side of Hotel Aulac in a Belle Époque-style building, near Château d'Ouchy.

39. Viruses, microbes, bad bacteria

SUN: Who are the enemies of the people on Earth, according to Dediu Method?

EARTH: The enemies of the people on Earth are not other people, but viruses, microbes, bad bacteria and hundreds of deadly illnesses – all people on Earth will work together against these real enemies for all of us.

Palazzo Giustinian (left), Piazza San Marco (center), Palazzo Ducale (center-right), seen from the east end of Canal Grande.

40. Non-violence

SUN: How do you establish non-violence, using Dediu Method?

EARTH: Non-violence is a strict requirement for all activities on Earth. The first rule for everybody on Earth comes from the Hippocratic Oath: Primum non nocere - first do not harm.

SUN: How will the doctors help?

EARTH: Medical doctors and assistants will make regular home visits to all people, to keep them healthy, and to prevent illnesses.

Italy, Venice from vaporetto, with Il Campanile di San Marco in the middle.

41. Truth

SUN: Truth is a big problem – how do you apply Dediu Method?

EARTH: People need only truth in order to create a long term peaceful and harmonious society.

SUN: And if someone lies?

EARTH: If someone lies – medical treatment will follow.

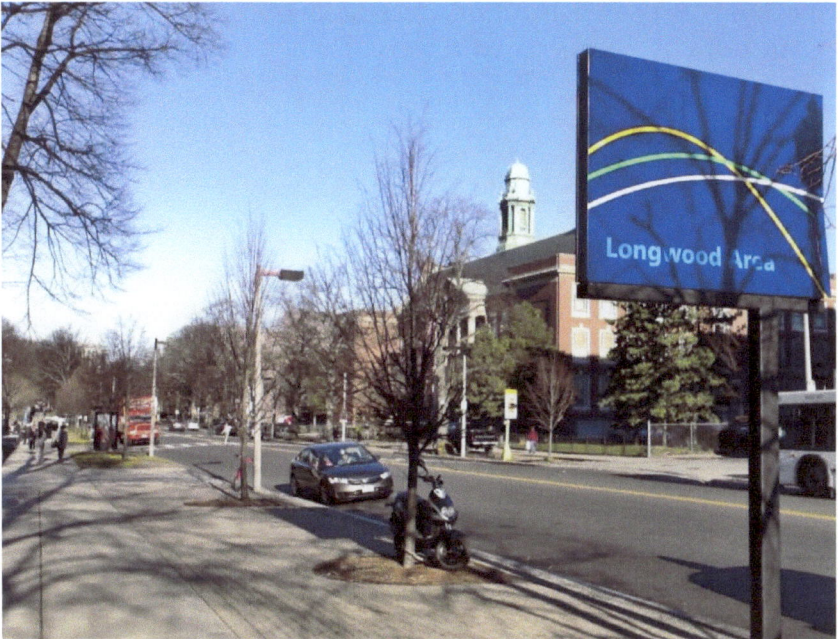

USA, Boston: 3 Dec 2009, on Avenue Louis Pasteur (1822-1895, French microbiologist), looking northeast to Boston Public Latin School (1635, Schola Latina Bostoniensis, center right) in Longwood Area.

42. Fundamental requirement

SUN: What about freedom, using Dediu Method?

EARTH: Yes, freedom is a fundamental requirement on Earth.

SUN: Does freedom mean that everybody does what they want?

EARTH: No, it is well understood that this freedom refers to doing good things in a civilized manner, not for war, violence or similar bad things, which are against the wellbeing of the people.
Freedom goes hand in hand with responsibility.
People can assemble peacefully only.

Switzerland: From Genève to Thoiry (France), on Route de Meyrin, 2 km west from Geneva Cointrin Airport, there is this renovation of the external structural Elements of the Globe of Science and Innovation.

43. Economy

SUN: Economy – how will it be, according to Dediu Method?

EARTH: For economy it is clear that the free market economy, while not perfect, gives the best results, but all people will have the option to choose between friendly private services, and friendly government services. Independent assistants and monitors will make sure that there are no abuses. Sine qua non requirements for happiness are morality and free market.

SUN: And religion?

EARTH: The religion will be free, and is expected not to interfere with activities of the Advisors, and actually should help people.

SUN: Can you petition the Government?

EARTH: People of course can petition the small Word Government, and can change it anytime, if it does not perform as expected.

44. Budget surplus

SUN: Budget deficits are common for governments – how do you apply Dediu Method?

EARTH: All budgets will have a surplus of 2% - there will be a strict application of the Latin aphorism: "Sumptus censum ne superset" (Let not your spending exceed your income).

Italy, Venezia: San Theodore Column (left), Basilica di San Marco (back), Palazzo Ducale, Lion of Venice Column (right).

45. Correcting errors

SUN: There are plenty of errors everywhere – what you do about this?

EARTH: Correcting errors is a permanent duty for everybody - Darwin (circa 140 years ago, around 1880) said "To kill an error is as good a service as, and sometimes even better than, the establishing of a new truth or fact."

France: From Geneva to Mont Blanc (4810 m) on freeway A40, near Cluses, with Le Grand Bornand Mountain (left back).

46. Kindness

SUN: Well, kindness is really good, right?

EARTH: Kindness is a requirement for everybody.
Seneca (circa 1,960 years ago) said "Wherever there is a human being, there is an opportunity for a kindness."
This is a fundamental idea which must be constantly applied.

Switzerland, Lausanne (Roman 150, 147,000, 41 km^2, 500 m elevation, 62 km northeast of Geneva, the home of the International Olympic Committee), near Château d'Ouchy (1170, 1609, 1893).

47. Highly mobile

SUN: Governments are usually fix in their old massive buildings –
how will this change using Dediu Method?

EARTH: All levels of government will be highly mobile - changing
of the capitals for the 10 regions, and for the 100 sub-regions, etc.
It is necessary to move the government close to the people, to be
able to quickly solve the local problems.
Locally the people will decide how to better organize themselves, to
be more efficient and harmonious, with the help of the world
government when necessary. Like in any big family, there will be
differences in organization and management, based on their abilities
and objectives, but all must be peaceful and harmonious. Conflicts
will be promptly resolved by the medical personnel, police, and
other assistants.

Italy, Venezia: Palazzi Mocenigo (right), Corner-Spinelli (center),
Benzon, Volpi, north bank, north-east direction, 1.35 km west of
San Marco.

48. World Police and Assistance

SUN: The Police Department is always necessary – what changes will you have?

EARTH: The United Nations will change in 2-3 years (for example, by 2024) into World Police and Assistance Organization (WPAO), to help local police in case of big natural disasters or big accidents, and will report to the top 10 Advisers. They will be located in all capitals, and help the locals. When an emergency appears, they will quickly move to solve the emergency.

The police powers will be limited, and they will know and be friend with all the people in their jurisdiction – this is the key element of a civilized and peaceful Earth. If they notice a person with bad intentions, they immediately retain that person and call for a medical assistant (and other assistants, if necessary), to analyze and solve the issue very quickly.

Police will be people's friends everywhere, and they will always help people.

USA, the University of California, Berkeley (1868, named after the philosopher and mathematician Bishop George Berkeley (1685-1753), motto Fiat lux (Let there be light), 36,200 students, 72 Nobel laureates, 500 ha campus), Physics Department in Le Conte Hall (1924, center), Campanile (back (61 bells (full concert carillon) and clock tower). 1914, 94 m, 7 floors, observation deck on the 8th floor, inspired by il Campanile (850, 1514, 1912, 99 m) di San Marco (1084), Venezia (421, Venice), Italy (900 BC)).

49. Prevention

SUN: Prevention of bad events is really difficult – what is your approach?

EARTH: Prevention of bad events is the main objective of everybody. If a bad event occurs, the police and their assistants will eliminate the consequences, reestablish the normal situation, and determine why the bad event occurred, in order to improve their activity, and prevent such bad events in the future.

Private property cannot be taken for public use, without just compensation, decided by at least 5 assistants.

A person cannot be deprived by government of life, liberty, or property, without having several doctors and other assistants agree: for life – at least 12; for liberty – at least 6; for property – at least 3. A person cannot deprive another person of life, liberty, or property, which, unfortunately, occurs very frequently in the world, and very much effort and energy will be allocated to prevent such bad events. In order to prevent bad things, the police, doctors and their assistants will be in permanent contact with all the people, by visiting them, phone calls, e-mails, tele-videos, and mail, to keep everybody calm and happy.

9 May 2013, Finland, Helsinki: beautiful buildings on Mikonkatu, with Aleksi store, close to Aleksanterinkatu, 200 m south-east of the Helsinki Central Railway Station.

50. Non-stop working

SUN: You know, about 66% of the people of the world are working at any moment.

EARTH: Yes, therefore, non-stop working of all world government departments – especially medical, police, emergency, volunteers – will be carefully organized.

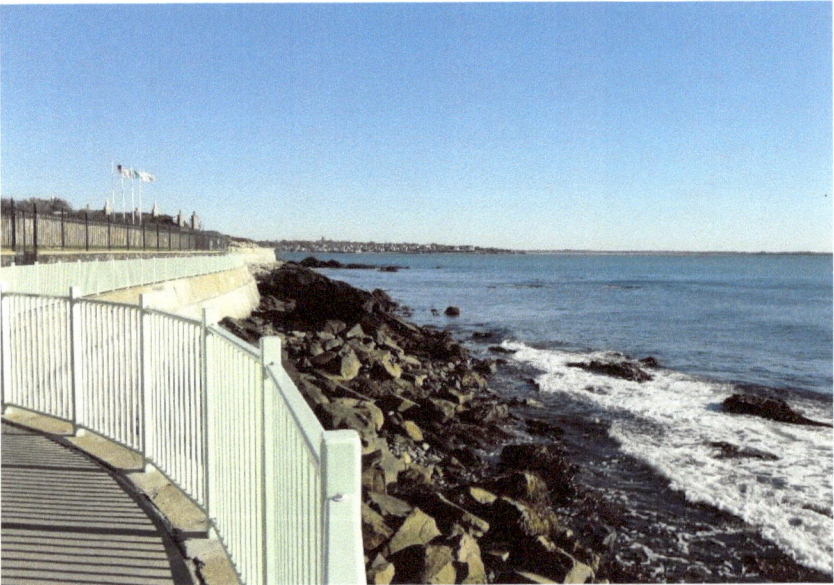

USA, Newport, RI: Cliff Walk (1985, 5.6 km, public access walkway that borders the Atlantic shore line, looking north, with the Easton Bay on the right).

51. Privacy

SUN: Privacy of discussions is a necessity.

EARTH: Indeed, in order to have serious and constructive discussions and negotiations, they must be private. Privacy and discipline are necessary for good government work. The results will be public and preserved, but not the private discussions.

Italy, Venezia: Libreria (left), San Theodore Column, Palazzo Ducale, Lion of Venice Column (center) on Riva degli Schiavoni street.

52. Politeness

SUN: Politeness is so beautiful.

EARTH: Of course, and it is a strict requirement for the top management, and for all others, to be highly civilized, polite, courteous, harmonious and efficient. Who wants to work for the world government must have good manners. Harmony in the world starts from the harmony and good manners of the people in the world government.

Switzerland, Geneva, on Quai du Mont Blanc, Beau Rivage Hotel (right, 1865, Mayer family, in 1918 Czechoslovakia creation document signed).

53. No conflicts

SUN: Volens, nolens, conflicts frequently appear.

EARTH: True – however, all conflicts must not only be quickly resolved, but they must be transformed in friendships. This is very important for long term stability. The medical personnel and others will work diligently to make sure that disputes are resolved, and then a friendship is developed. Only in this way the situation will become stable. People want peace, freedom, health, friendship and prosperity, therefore conflicts should be quickly resolved, and then the corrective medical treatment will include the transformation of hostility and aggressiveness into harmony and friendship.

Italy, Venezia: Palazzo Corner-Spinelli (left), Fermata Sant' Angelo, and other lovely buildings, north bank, 1.5 km west of San Marco.

54. Easy communication

SUN: Easy communication between all people is a high priority.

EARTH: Certainly, as a single big, over 7.7 B, family on Earth, all people must be able to communicate easily with each other. For this reason, a common language and alphabet on Earth are needed. Because English is a de facto common language now, it will be taken as the basis of the world language, let's call it Mundo, which will be taught in all schools, and used in the world government. All the other languages will continue as secondary languages. The same is true for the Latin alphabet, which will be used everywhere, with other alphabets as secondary. The teachers will have a very significant role in implementing this.

Switzerland, Geneva, Restaurant Vieux-Bois, Avenue de la Paix, 150 m west from the Palace of Nations and 150 m southwest from the Red Cross.

USA, New York: On West 42nd St at Fifth Avenue, looking at Chrysler building (back up, Walter P. Chrysler (1875-1940), 1930, 319 m, 77 floors, 111,000 m^2 floor area, 32 elevators, at Lexington Ave.), before it is Grand Hyatt New York Hotel (1919, 90 m), and before it is Grand Central Terminal (1871, 1903, 1913, 2000, built by Cornelius Vanderbilt (1794-1877, the 2nd richest American, after John D. Rockefeller (1839-1937)) and his 13 children, commuter railroad terminal, with a grand façade and concourse, at Park Avenue, 47 acres, 44 high-level platforms, 67 tracks on 2 levels).

55. Global wealth

SUN: Global wealth is not too bad.

EARTH: Indeed, the 2018 Global Wealth Report from Credit Suisse shows that the total global wealth has reached $317 trillions (circa $41,000/person), which is encouraging, and all this wealth must be used only for peace.

Like in any big family, there are differences, because some work more, some spend less, some move faster, and, especially, some are sick – this is the main reason for differences: not all people can be equally sick, some people are sicker than others. However, all the people and the government will work to help each other.

It is a major responsibility of the Government to increase the global wealth, and to train those in need, to have better working abilities and opportunities.

Switzerland, Geneva, on Pont du Mont Blanc (1862, 1965, 252 m X 26.8 m, over Rhône river), going northwest, Les Bergues Hotel (1834) (center).

56. No bureaucracy

SUN: Bureaucracy is always a big issue.

EARTH: And the response is no bureaucracy – this is required by all people, and every day attention will be given for improvements in this direction. In a well-organized country, with all people working together in harmony, this can be accomplished in several years.

Italy, Venezia: Giardinetti Reali (Royal Gardens, left), Libreria Sansoviniana, Il Campanile, Palazzo Ducale, Riva degli Schiavoni street.

57. No duplication

SUN: Corruption and duplication also need attention.

EARTH: Sure, everybody will work really hard to completely eliminate corruption, organized crime and drug trafficking. Constant attention will be focused on avoiding duplication at all levels of the world government – there must be continuous collaboration between all levels, to prevent duplication, and to eliminate it, if it was found.

USA, Newport, RI: The Breakers, 1893-1895, built by Cornelius Vanderbilt II (1843-1899), 70 rooms, gross area 11,644 m^2, living area 5,804 m^2 on 5 floors, house footprint an acre (4,047 m^2), 9.1 m sculpted iron gates.

58. Reserves and savings

SUN: Good reserves and savings are welcome.

EARTH: Certainly, each government department will have some reserves for special situations (natural disasters, big accidents), and the banks will also have good financial reserves. All people will be encouraged to save some money in banks with 5% interest.

Switzerland, Geneva, from Quai Gustave Ador (1845-1928, President). Jet d'Eau – a large fountain pumping water at 0.5 m^3/s to 140 m, lit up at night.

59. Integrity and efficiency

SUN: Integrity and efficiency can always be a little better.

EARTH: Right, inspectors will help the Government with the integrity and efficiency issues – always there are ways to improve the work. Inspectors will give advice regarding integrity and efficiency, and will take corrective actions when necessary.

Italy, Venezia: Palazzo Giustinian (center), Calle Ridotto (right), Calle 13 Martiri (left) and Rio Moise (left), 300 m south-west from San Marco.

60. Family assistance

SUN: First thing first: family assistance.

EARTH: No question about this. Because all families need assistance from time to time, and the big 7.7 B family on Earth contains billions of small families, all of them will have the assistance they need – this will be the result of one country well organized and managed.

USA, Newport, RI: Chateau-sur-Mer, 1851, 17 acres, William Shepard Wetmore (1801-1862, a merchant in the China trade)

61. Harmony

SUN: Harmony can be achieved.

EARTH: Sure - because all people on Earth want to live in harmony right now, it will be relatively easy to implement this in one good and civilized country. This may include having small, beautiful and commonly agreed fences around properties, because good fences make good neighbors, and also helps with more privacy.

Switzerland, Geneva (121 BC under Romans), Avenue de la Paix 19, International Committee of the Red Cross, founded by Jean Henri Dunant (1828-1910) on Feb. 9, 1863, three Nobel Peace Prizes.

62. Dispute resolution

SUN: Volens nolens disputes appear, and dispute resolution is required.

EARTH: Of course, and dispute resolution is not only Government's obligation, but it will be everybody's duty. There will be professional assistance from medical personnel, police, people assistance specialists, volunteers, religious organizations, and many others, but the bottom line is that everybody must avoid disputes.

When there are different opinions, just stay calm, express your opinion, listen to others, and continue calm the discussion until a compromise is reached. There is no need to spend much time and energy – let the people decide, and even if your idea is not temporarily accepted, there are chances that in the future you'll have more people agree with you.

USA, Newport: Osgood-Pell House, 1888, (William H. Osgood (1830-1896, zinc)), from 1992 office for The Preservation Society of Newport County.

63. No abuses

SUN: Well, power creates conditions for abuses, which must be corrected.

EARTH: Indeed, special attention will be given by Advisors to avoid abuses and wrong interpretations of the rules. All assistants (doctors, mathematicians, CEOs, engineers and teachers) will closely monitor all activities, to avoid abuses and wrong interpretations of the rules. This requirement of not having abuses is demanding – but this is a general job, not only for Government, but for everybody, as part of the big family, we just don't need abuses.

The abuse, in some places, of confiscating the land by some government bureaucrats, will be eliminated – the land belongs to the people, not the government.

The abuse, in some places, of having trains, airplanes, and others making unhealthy noises, with the government support, will be eliminated – peoples' health has always priority.

The abuse, in some places, of having to change the clocks twice a year will be eliminated – only the normal local time zones will be used.

If abuses are observed, they will be immediately reported to the Government, and corrected, in general, by the People Assistance Department, which will have personnel, including medical assistants, to analyze and promptly solve the abuses.

London: From Kennington Road (to right) at Westminster Bridge Road (left), looking southeast to Oasis Academy, South Bank (left down), and Oasis Church Waterloo (1783, 1985, Baptist). Just 50 m south (to left) of Lambeth North Station (for the underground Waterloo line, between Elephant & Castle and Waterloo), 500 m south from the Waterloo Station (for trains and for subway), and 1 km southeast from the Westminster Bridge.

64. Free commerce

SUN: So beautiful – free commerce, speech, press!

EARTH: True - in one country, with one market, the commerce between the people on Earth will be free of taxes, tariffs, duties, etc. – plenty of opportunities for everybody.

The speech will be free and responsible. It is expected not to call for war, violence, or similar destructive activities. People want peace, freedom, health, friendship and prosperity.

The press will be free and responsible. It is expected not to call for war, violence, or similar destructive activities. People want peace, freedom, health, friendship and prosperity.

People can assemble peacefully only, with police for help. It is expected not to call for war, violence, or similar destructive activities. People want peace, freedom, health, friendship and prosperity.

London, UK: From the Spur Rd, looking west to the Victoria Memorial (1911, 1924, right), and to the Buckingham Palace (1703, 1850, 1913, left).

65. Plenty of jobs

SUN: Will you have enough jobs?

EARTH: Yes, there will always be plenty of jobs at world minimum wage (assisting other people, for example), and the standard situation will be this: more jobs than available people, so people will choose the jobs they like the most.

No unemployment, no homelessness, no begging, no tipping – just all working harmoniously, having good houses, and helping each other.

USA, Boston, 3 Dec 2009, from Avenue Louis Pasteur (1822-1895, French microbiologist), Boston Public Latin School (1635, Schola Latina Bostoniensis, the oldest and the first public exam school in the U.S.).

Italy, Venice: The Clock Tower (Torre dell'Orologio), 1499. At the top - two bronze figures, which strike the hours on a bell. The bell was casted at the Arsenal in 1497. Below is the winged lion of Venice. There was a statue of the Doge Agostino Barbarigo (Doge 1486-1501) kneeling before the lion. Below the statues of the Virgin and Child. On either side are two large blue panels showing the time: 5:55 PM, the same on the clock below: XVII very close to XVIII.

66. Limited number of rules

SUN: The more rules, the less respect for them.

EARTH: It is well known – therefore all rules proposed by Advisers must be approved by their 5 assistants (doctors, mathematicians, CEOs, engineers and teachers), and for any new rule over 2,000 basic rules (each rule on at most half a page, total 1,000 pages), at least on old rule must be eliminated.

All the rules can be changed or eliminated when a majority of the people or their Advisors agree, but some fundamental peace and order rules will remain.

USA, Newport, RI: The southeast side of Isaac Bell (1846-1889, businessman and Ambassador to the Netherlands) House (Edna Villa), 1882, 4046 m^2.

67. Improvements

SUN: When the Constitution of the World can be changed?

EARTH: The Constitution of the World can be improved when 66% of the voters agree.

Italy, Venezia: Palazzo Giustinian (center), Calle Ridotto (right), Calle 13 Martiri (left) and Rio Moise (left), 330 m south-west from San Marco.

68. Purpose

SUN: Therefore, what is the purpose for all people on Earth?

EARTH: The purpose for all people on Earth is to be healthy, to live in peace, freedom and harmony, to be prosperous, and to prepare to expand to the Moon, asteroids, Mars, and other places in the Universe, which can support life.

USA, Newport, RI: The south side of the west part of Kingscote, 1839 (George Noble Jones (1811 – 1876)), Gothic Revival mansion near Bellevue Ave.

69. Immediate objectives

SUN: Do you have immediate objectives for everybody?

EARTH: Important immediate objectives for everybody are:
- Reserve time for happiness.
- Use robots and automated processes, work less, and spend more time with your family.
- The weekend will be like a small vacation.
- Prevent burnout.
- Make civilized behavior and harmony everywhere an important issue.
- Eliminate stress.
- Help friends and colleagues.
- Keep everybody relaxed, calm, friendly, patient, and happy.

Italy, Venezia: Palazzo Treves de Bonfili (right) on Rio Moise (right), Palazzo Tiepolo (center), north bank, 350 m west from San Marco.

70. Starting this new structure

SUN: Any idea how to start this new structure of the world?

EARTH: To start this new structure of the world, one idea could be this: the first Honorific World Observer (from UN, for example) could invite 10 Presidents form big countries (like USA, China, Russia, UK, India, France, Japan, Germany, Brasil, and Egypt) to be the first 10 Advisors Level 4, starting, for example, on January 1st, 2021, for 10 months, until November 1st, 2021, when the new calm and noiseless elections will take place. The same for the 100 Advisers Level 3, and so on.

22 Nov 2008, looking south to the north façade of Kawaguchiko Station (on the Fujikyu Kawaguchiko Line, terminal station, moving only to the left (southeast)) and the northern side of Mount Fuji (3,776 m, 1707 last eruption).

71. Where the Constitution of the World is in force

SUN: And where the Constitution of the World is in force?

EARTH: The Constitution of the World is in force not only on Earth, but also in the space around Earth, on the Moon, Mars, asteroids and any other places were the very good people on Earth will be moving in the future.

Italy, Venezia: Palazzo Corner (Ca' Granda) (Prefettura) (left), and two pretty houses (right), with Rio di San Maurizio between them, north bank.

72. When? We cannot wait!

SUN: Any time limitations?

EARTH: The Constitution of the World is intended for at least 10,000 years of harmonious living on the happy Earth.

The Constitution of the World is ready to come into force, and to be put into practice, for the benefit of all people on Earth, on 6 March 2020, and it is ready to remain into force, and enjoyed by all people at least until 6 March 12020.

USA, Newport, RI: The west site of the Elms, 1899 - 1901, Edward Julius Berwind (1848 – 1936), from Château d'Asnières (1753) in Asnières-sur-Seine (1158, 7.9 km northwest of the center of Paris, France).

Bibliography

"The Histories" by Polybius
"Discours de la Méthode" by René Descartes
"Meditationes de prima philosophia" by René Descartes
"Philosophiae Naturalis Principia Mathematica" by Isaac Newton
Chinese encyclopedia Gujin Tushu Jicheng (Imperial Encyclopedia)
"Encyclopédie" by Jean-Baptiste le Rond d'Alembert and Denis Diderot
"Encyclopaedia Britannica" by over 4,400 contributors
"Encyclopedia Americana" by Francis Lieber
Other sources include: UPI, CNBC, AP, Nasdaq, Reuters, EDGAR, AFP, Recode, Europa Press, Bloomberg News, Fox News, USA, Deutsche Presse-Agentur, MSNBC, BBC, Australian Associated Press, Agência Brasil, The Canadian Press (La Presse Canadienne), Middle East News Agency, Baltic News Service, Suomen Tietotoimisto, Athens-Macedonian News Agency, Asian News International, Inter Press Service, Kyodo News, Notimex, Algemeen Nederlands Persbureau, AGERPRES, Newsis, Tidningarnas Telegrambyrå, Swiss Telegraphic Agency, Central News Agency, ANKA news agency, Agenzia Fides

Michael M. Dediu is also the author of these books (which can be found on Amazon.com, and www.derc.com):

1. Aphorisms and quotations – with examples and explanations
2. Axioms, aphorisms and quotations – with examples and explanations
3. 100 Great Personalities and their Quotations
4. Professor Petre P. Teodorescu – A Great Mathematician and Engineer
5. Professor Ioan Goia – A Dedicated Engineering Professor
6. Venice (Venezia) – a new perspective. A short presentation with photographs
7. La Serenissima (Venice) - a new photographic perspective. A short presentation with many photos

8. Grand Canal – Venice. A new photographic viewpoint. A short presentation with many photos

9. Piazza San Marco – Venice. A different photographic view. A short presentation with many photos

10. Roma (Rome) - La Città Eterna. A new photographic view. A short presentation with many photos

11. Why is Rome so Fascinating? A short presentation with many photos

12. Rome, Boston and Helsinki. A short photographic presentation

13. Rome and Tokyo – two captivating cities. A short photographic presentation

14. Beautiful Places on Earth – A new photographic presentation

15. From Niagara Falls to Mount Fuji via Rome - A novel photographic presentation

16. From the USA and Canada to Italy and Japan - A fresh photographic presentation

17. Paris – Why So Many Call This City Mon Amour - A lovely photographic presentation

18. The City of Light – Paris (La Ville-Lumière) - A kaleidoscopic photographic presentation

19. Paris (Lutetia Parisiorum) – the romance capital of the world - A kaleidoscopic photographic view

20. Paris and Tokyo – a joyful photographic presentation. With a preamble about the Universe

21. From USA to Japan via Canada – A cheerful photographic documentary

22. 200 Wonderful Places, In The Last 50 Years – A personal photographic documentary

23. Must see places in USA and Japan - A kaleidoscopic photographic documentary

24. Grandeurs of the World - A kaleidoscopic photographic documentary

25. Corneliu Leu – writer on the same wavelength as Mark Twain. An American viewpoint

26. From Berkeley to Pompeii via Rome – A kaleidoscopic photographic documentary

27. From America to Europe via Japan - A kaleidoscopic photographic documentary

28. Discover America and Japan - A photographic documentary

29. J. R. Lucas – philosopher on a creative parallel with Plato, An American viewpoint

30. From America to Switzerland via France - A photographic documentary

31. From Bretton Woods to New York via Cape Cod - A photographic documentary

32. Splendid Places on the Atlantic Coast of the U. S. A. - A photographic documentary

33. Fourteen nice Cities on three Continents - A photographic documentary

34. 17 Picturesque Cities on the World Map - A photographic documentary

35. Unforgettable Places from Four Continents, including Trump buildings - A photographic documentary

36. Dediu Newsletter, Volume 1, Number 1, 6 December 2016 – Monthly news, review, comments and suggestions for a better and wiser world

37. Dediu Newsletter, Volume 1, Number 2, 6 January 2017 (available also at www.derc.com).

38. Dediu Newsletter, Volume 1, Number 3, 6 February 2017 (available at www.derc.com).

39. London and Greenwich, - A photographic documentary

40. Dediu Newsletter, Volume 1, Number 4, 6 March 2017 (available also at www.derc.com).

41. Dediu Newsletter, Volume 1, Number 5, 6 April 2017 (available also at www.derc.com).

42. Dediu Newsletter, Volume 1, Number 6, 6 May 2017 (available also at www.derc.com).

43. Dediu Newsletter, Volume 1, Number 7, 6 June 2017 (available also at www.derc.com).

44. London, Oxford and Cambridge, A photographic documentary

45. Dediu Newsletter, Volume 1, Number 8, 6 July 2017 (available also at www.derc.com).

46. Dediu Newsletter, Volume 1, Number 9, 6 August 2017 (available also at www.derc.com).

47. Dediu Newsletter, Volume 1, Number 10, 6 September 2017 (available also at www.derc.com).

Italy, Roma: Fontana di Trevi (1732 – 1762). Standing 26.3 m high and 49.15 m wide, it is located on Palazzo di Poli (1566). Tritons guide Oceanus' shell chariot, calming hippocampi. In the center an imaginatively modeled triumphal arch is placed over on the palazzo façade. The center niche, or exedra, framing Oceanus, has free-standing columns for greatest light and shade. Pietro Bracci's Oceanus (god of all water) is the central sculpture.

48. Three Great Professors: President Woodrow Wilson, Historian German Arciniegas, and Mathematician Gheorghe Vranceanu – A chronological and photographic documentary

49. Dediu Newsletter, Volume 1, Number 11, 6 October 2017 (available also at www.derc.com).

50. Dediu Newsletter, Volume 1, Number 12, 6 November 2017 (available also at www.derc.com).

51. Dediu Newsletter, Volume 2, Number 1 (13), 6 December 2017 (available also at www.derc.com).

52. Two Great Leaders: Augustus and George Washington - A chronological and photographic documentary

53. Dediu Newsletter, Volume 2, Number 2 (14), 6 January 2018 (available also at www.derc.com).

54. Newton, Benjamin Franklin, and Gauss, A chronological and photographic documentary

55. Dediu Newsletter, Volume 2, Number 3 (15), 6 February 2018 (available also at www.derc.com).

56. 2017: World Top Events, But Many Little Known, A chronological and photographic documentary

57. Dediu Newsletter, Volume 2, Number 4 (16), 6 March 2018 (available also at www.derc.com).

58. Vergilius, Horatius, Ovidius, and Shakespeare - A chronological and photographic documentary.

59. Dediu Newsletter, Volume 2, Number 5 (17), 6 April 2018 (available also at www.derc.com).

60. Dediu Newsletter, Volume 2, Number 6 (18), 6 May 2018 (available also at www.derc.com).

61. Vivaldi, Bach, Mozart, and Verdi - A chronological and photographic documentary.

62. Dediu Newsletter, Volume 2, Number 7 (19), 6 June 2018 (available also at www.derc.com).

63. Dediu Newsletter, Volume 2, Number 8 (20), 6 July 2018 (available also at www.derc.com).

64. Dediu Newsletter, Volume 2, Number 9 (21), 6 August 2018 (available also at www.derc.com).

65. World History, a new perspective - A chronological and photographic documentary.

66. World Humor History with over 100 Jokes, a new perspective - A chronological and photographic documentary

67. Dediu Newsletter, Volume 2, Number 10 (22), 6 September 2018 (available also at www.derc.com).

68. Dediu Newsletter, Volume 2, Number 11 (23), 6 October 2018 (available also at www.derc.com).

69. Dediu Newsletter, Volume 2, Number 12 (24), 6 November 2018

70. Da Vinci, Michelangelo, Rembrandt, Rodin - A chronological and photographic documentary

71. Dediu Newsletter, Volume 3, Number 1 (25), 6 December 2018

72. Dediu Newsletter, Volume 3, Number 2 (26), 6 January 2019

73. From Euclid to Edison – revelries in the past 75 years - A chronological and photographic documentary

74. – Socrates to Churchill Aphorisms celebrated after 1960 - A chronological and photographic documentary

75. - Dediu Newsletter, Volume 3, Number 3 (27), 6 February 2019

76. – Hippocrates to Fleming: Medicine History celebrated after 1943 - A chronological and photographic documentary

77. - Dediu Newsletter, Volume 3, Number 4 (28), 6 March 2019

78. - Dediu Newsletter, Volume 3, Number 5 (29), 6 April 2019

79 – Archimedes to Ford: Invention History celebrated after 1943 - A chronological and photographic documentary

80 - Dediu Newsletter, Volume 3, Number 6 (30), 6 May 2019

81 – Sutherland to Pavarotti: Great Singers History - A chronological and photographic documentary

82 - Dediu Newsletter, Volume 3, Number 7 (31), 6 June 2019

83 - Dediu Newsletter, Volume 3, Number 8 (32), 6 July 2019

84 – Augustus to Rockefeller: History of the Wealthiest People - A chronological and photographic documentary

85 - Dediu Newsletter, Volume 3, Number 9 (33), 6 August 2019

86 – Pythagoras to Fermi: History of Science - A chronological and photographic documentary

87 - Dediu Newsletter, Volume 3, Number 10 (34), 6 September 2019

88 – Our Future is Sustainable Peace and Prosperity – Moving from conflicts to harmony and peace

89 - Dediu Newsletter, Volume 3, Number 11 (35), 6 October 2019 – World Monthly Report with news

90 – Our Future Depends on Good World Educations – Moving from frail education to solid education

91 - Dediu Newsletter, Volume 3, Number 12 (36), 6 November 2019 – World Monthly Report with News and Suggestions for Sustainable Peace, Freedom and Prosperity

92 – Friendly, Helpful & Smart World Management - Moving from bureaucracy to responsive world management

93 – If You Want Peace, Prepare for Peace! – Moving from preparation for war to preparation for peace

94 - Dediu Newsletter, Volume 4, Number 1 (37), 6 December 2019 – World Monthly Report with News and Suggestions for Sustainable Peace, Freedom and Prosperity

95 – World with One Country & its Ten Friendly Regions - Moving from 195 disagreeing countries, to 1 country with 10 collaborating regions

96 - Dediu Newsletter, Volume 4, Number 2 (38), 6 January 2020 – World Monthly Report with News and Suggestions for Sustainable Peace, Freedom and Prosperity

97 – After 10,000 Years of Conflicts, People want 10,000 Years of Harmony - Moving from continuous wars to stable peace

98 - Dediu Newsletter, Volume 4, Number 3 (39), 6 February 2020 – World Monthly Report with News and Suggestions for Sustainable Peace, Freedom and Prosperity

99 - Dediu Newsletter, Volume 4, Number 4 (40), 6 March 2020 – World Monthly Report with News and Suggestions for Sustainable Peace, Freedom and Prosperity

100 - Dediu Newsletter, Volume 4, Number 5 (41), 6 April 2020 – World Monthly Report

101 - Dediu Newsletter, Volume 4, Number 6 (42), 6 May 2020 – World Monthly Report

••

Auspicium Melioris Aevi (Hope of a better age)

Italy, Venezia: In the middle of the west façade of the Basilica di San Marco, we see the central bronze-fashioned door, in a round-arched portal, encircled by polychrome marble columns. Above this door there are three round bas-relief cycles of Romanesque art. A Japanese couple, with their Japanese photographer, make their wedding photographs in this most beautiful place.